CONTENTS

FOREWORD

I first met Evelyn Schaffer when I was Deputy Chief of Dunbarton-shire Constabulary and she paid a visit to Force headquarters. It was obvious that she was tremendously interested in policing; particularly in the relationship between the police and the community: the pillar on which British policing depends for its effectiveness. That common interest and concern was the cement which formed a bond of friendship between us. Later when I became Chief Constable of Strathclyde she was of immense help in setting up a new Community Involvement Branch.

Her understanding and no-nonsense approach to the problems and pressures of modern policing continually impress me. She knows as much about policing as any psychologist in Britain today; a fact which is amply demonstrated throughout this book.

Having recently enlisted her aid once again, this time as a member of a committee who are reviewing Metropolitan Police recruitment and training, I was especially interested in the chapter on Training. Whilst Evelyn Schaffer is right when she says in the Introduction that I may not agree with all she says, in discussing police training she gives voice to much of my own dissatisfaction with the efficacy of our present training system, particularly with regard to the way in which we train our new officers. As society changes so must the police service respond to that change; so must police training reflect the needs of our modern urban society.

In writing this book Evelyn Schaffer has made a valuable contribution to the continuing debate about modern policing. I recommend it as compulsory reading for every new recruit to the police service. It will give him or her an invaluable perspective about their job. For more experienced and senior police officers the book underlines the essential philosophy of British policing and reminds us how important it is that we remain a part of the community and not apart from it. To members of that community let me say that this book raises questions and provides insights that could only have been written by someone with a true sympathy for and understanding of the British police service—warts and all.

Sir David McNee

PREFACE

This book is a view of the police written by an outsider who has worked very closely with the police. I have tried to cover as many different Forces and projects as possible but inevitably many are not mentioned. When illustrating particular procedures I have selected the larger, urban forces, working on the principle that if community projects can survive in urban environments, they will survive anywhere. There is a great deal about Scotland. This is because Scotland pioneered community policing. This was due to two men—David Gray who, as Chief Constable of Greenock, started the first community policing projects and, as HM Chief Inspector of Constabulary, has continued to promote all aspects of community policing; and David McNee who, as first Chief Constable of Strathclyde Police, the largest force in Scotland and the second largest in Britain, took over some of David Gray's ideas and added some of his own, giving Strathclyde police the most sophisticated Community Involvement Branch in the UK. I owe thanks to both Mr Gray and Sir David, who may not approve of all I have written but encouraged me to do it. My thanks also go to Chief Superintendent Robert Fraser of Strathclyde Police and Superintendent John Newing of the Metropolitan Police, who so generously gave of their time to read parts of the book and who have made many helpful suggestions which are incorporated in the text; to the Greater Glasgow Health Board, my employers, who have patiently tolerated my involvement with the police; to the Winston Churchill Memorial Trust and the Council of Europe, who financed visits to police forces in the USA, Canada, Norway and Sweden; to the girls who typed the scripts; and, most of all, to the many police officers who, knowingly and unknowingly, contributed most of the ideas written in this book.

1 INTRODUCTION

What is law and order? Who should be responsible for the maintenance of law and order in society? How can this onerous task best be done? The answers to these questions are not so simple as it may first appear and present the community with one of its greatest challenges; answers given by various sectional interests cause more emotional heat than almost any other subject. They are a trap in which society is caught because of the belief that there is an answer to be found. The pendulum of public opinion swings between 'hard' and 'soft' lines, expecting quick results from what are usually half-hearted measures; The Social Work (Scotland) Act, 1968 and the corresponding 1969 Act in England being good examples. The philosophy of these Acts was sound and showed tremendous progress in thinking about juvenile offending and the needs of children; sadly, the back-up facilities and support provided were no different to that which already existed, were maybe rather poorer, as a result of which the Acts have been brought into disrepute, regarded as failures.

Some believe that if we are tough enough on criminals, they will be deterred from crime; others that, if only we cease from being tough and show that we care, crime will drop. From time to time, some cause will become fashionable and legislation will be introduced to deal with it, legislation that is usually based on either political expediency or idealism. It was once considered that poverty caused crime and if we cleared up poverty, crime would disappear. Poverty is, in fact, still with us but is greatly reduced; it is not the widespread evil it was thirty years ago, but crime still escalates. Labelling young children as delinquent was considered to make them more likely to develop criminal tendencies, so take them out of the criminal justice system and juvenile offending would disappear. The problem has not gone away—indeed, in some areas it has actually been aggravated. No one would deny that poverty sometimes causes crime nor that some children are driven into crime through mishandling by authority, but few believe that either factor possesses the key to the problem of crime in society. Two popular platforms

11

for reformers are either 'lock more people up and for longer periods' or 'do not lock people up and release those who are locked up more quickly'. In Scotland they lock up more people per head of population than any other European country but they still have an escalating crime rate, higher than most. In Sweden the number of people locked up is very small and periods of imprisonment are shorter, but the level of criminality is the same as in the USA.

The difficulty is that very few people have the opportunity of seeing the whole spectrum of the criminal field and theories are developed from particular instances and personal experiences, well laced with rather primitive emotions. The average member of the community only knows about crime from what he reads in the paper or sees on TV, and we will discuss the role the media play later. A policeman is usually in at the first stage and sees the impact of an offence on the victims, but does not follow through the offender and so sometimes gets a rather distorted view. Lawyers and judges get a very limited and rather unrealistic view from the courts. The social worker tends to see another side of the offender, his problems and pressures, which sometimes leads to a deserved, sometimes to a distorted, compassion. Prison staff see yet another, and frequently a very degraded, side of the offender. In addition, many people have themselves been involved in anti-social behaviour at some time in their lives. For some it has been a trivial matter, they have not been caught and they prefer to forget, becoming rather intolerant of other people who get caught up in anti-social behaviour.

The motor car is responsible for a great deal of crime in society and has caused a wide spectrum of people to become involved with the police and courts. Many road traffic offenders rationalise their behaviour by criticisms of the police who, they consider, should deal with 'real' crime. They forget that speeding, thoughtless parking and careless driving may have consequences just as damaging as housebreaking or petty pilfering; that 10 per cent of hospital beds contain the victims of road traffic accidents and 30 per cent of deaths in the 15-25 age bracket are a result of traffic accidents. Most people continue to commit minor offences throughout their lives, fiddling their tax, using the office telephone for personal calls, using office stationery, fraudulently claiming expenses and a multitude of traffic offences. If challenged, they will defend themselves by saying 'everyone does it—no one really gets hurt, it's not real crime'. 'Real crime', and by this one inevitably means crime in which someone is caught, is, in fact, frequently very petty, involving little in financial terms, although the commensurate suffering caused to victims can be out of all proportion. It is nevertheless important to remember that serious crime, robbery, assault, murder etc., accounts for barely 10 per cent of crime committed and in a great deal of crime the victims are anonymous, large business concerns, local authorities, etc.—or there are no directly identifiable victims at all. This does not justify criminal activity but it does indicate that the 'trivial' everyday offending in which most people are involved does not differ greatly from the offending which is detected.

There is no simple answer to the problem of how to deal with crime, of how to stop its alarming escalation. Such an admission is itself very unsettling and maybe rather frightening. People feel so much more secure if they can hold on to the idea that there is a solution and the only reason it has not worked is that it has never been given a chance. To suggest that the problem is so great and complicated as to be almost insoluble, and that there are certainly no quick or simple answers, raises the frightening spectre of a 'breakdown of law and order' and a threat to everyone's way of life. The problem must be seen as soluble for the peace of mind of the community, it must be dealt with, not by 'us' the community, but by 'them', and 'them' usually means the police and the courts. When things get bad the general feeling tends to be that 'we' must put pressure on 'them'—that 'we' can do nothing ourselves. The fact that it is our children, friends, family, neighbours and staff that are involved is something that tends to be forgotten.

The police get caught between conflicting philosophies and are as involved in contributing to these philosophies as any other member of the community. They are bound to administer laws which they sometimes regard as absurd or even objectionable, but they lack the right to protest or abdicate their responsibility, a right which every other member of the community has in full.

Policing the countryside in Britain was, until the early nineteenth century, a direct community responsibility. Local 'constables' were appointed to maintain order and were responsible to the local dignitaries. The Army was called in to deal with civil riots but, as the Industrial Revolution progressed, bringing great changes to the dominantly rural communities, it became increasingly clear that controlling the civilian population was not a role for the Army. During some of the Chartist riots the level of civilian casualties was very high and the Army caused as many problems as it cured. The growing urban conurbations needed another form of control in order to maintain law and order. Parliament was very reluctant to accept Sir Robert Peel's plans for a police force but, as industrial unrest increased, finally gave in and one of the first police forces was established in 1829. This police force was instructed to make the streets safe by patrolling, and great emphasis was laid on the importance of winning public goodwill and support by operating under strict rules. The police were authorised to deal with the 'dangerous classes' and with political agitators.

At first everything went well as the police were successful in restoring order to the streets, they dealt effectively with the 'dangerous classes' and, best of all, they removed the responsibility for dealing with the problem of crime and disorder from the shoulders of the ordinary citizens who could now forget about such unpleasant matters. Their involvement with the problems of industrial unrest, the Chartists and the 'dangerous classes' inevitably made the police force appear to some as a tool of the bosses and the monied classes. Crime was confined to certain deprived areas of cities, it was regarded as very much an activity of the poor and vagrant and had nothing to do with respectable people. All very safe and cosy and, apparently, successful. However, no social situation is ever static and the nineteenth century was a period of particularly rapid and dramatic social change. Industrialisation was proceeding at a tremendous pace and causing havoc to many lives; cities were spreading like a stain across the countryside and small, familiar rural communities were rapidly being swallowed up in black smoke, factories, mills and slums. With the development of industry and the railways, people became more and more mobile and little communities began to change. These developments continued into the twentieth century when the enormous lateral growth of cities, accompanied by the development of the motor car, railways and other forms of public transport produced the great, anonymous industrialised conurbations which we have today.

Initially, therefore, the role of the police in Britain was reasonably clearly defined. The new force was not particularly popular with the working classes but it was tolerated within certain limits. Some areas of the cities remained fairly lawless and were rarely penetrated by the 'Peelers' except in search of particular quarry. The police rarely, if ever, penetrated the respectable drawing rooms of the merchants and propertied classes from whom they received warm and enthusiastic support—at a suitable distance. It was not surprising that the police were regarded as the tools of the rich and privileged and came to be regarded with increasing suspicion by the working classes—particularly in view of their role in dealing with the Chartist and other similar disturbances. As social and class distinctions became more blurred, so police activity impinged more and more on the privileged classes and police popularity waned there.

It is inevitable that a police service should not be particularly popular, even if it were possible to have sufficient men to give a personalised service, the 'village bobby' of fond memory. A policeman is associated with the community's weaknesses, troubles and failings, he is the person who witnesses the side of life that most people prefer to forget and from which most will disassociate themselves; violence, greed and every human weakness are part of the policeman's daily lot. When we meet a doctor we tend to think of our health and our various physical ailments, so when we come into contact with the police we tend to remember our weaknesses and failings and hope that the police do not know about them. This does not make for easy social relationships. It is inherent in the role which the police play that there will be tension between them and ordinary members of the community. On the other hand, the police, because they see the seamy side of the community, because they are involved in dealing with the sad and petty weaknesses, the cruelty and selfishness of individuals, tend to become rather cynical about their fellow citizens. We all generalise from our personal experiences, and the experiences of the average policeman are such that they will inevitably affect his view of his fellow citizens, making him somewhat cynical.

In the days when communities were small and cities had not developed as anonymously as in recent times, most people knew their local policeman. Relationships were often good and it was possible to administer law in a personal way without constant resort to officialdom. A child caught pinching apples, shoplifting, dodging school, etc. was dealt with by the local policeman who was likely to be known and respected in the community. He would be able to handle the complaint in a manner which satisfied everyone, including both offender and complainant. A telling-off for the child and the assurance of parental action and that was usually the end of the matter. In modern society such incidents cannot be handled to anyone's satisfaction, injustice is always seen by one side or the other, often by both, and the police are seen as the individuals to be blamed by all involved. Parents and children know their rights and are often united in their opposition to the policeman who is dealing with a complaint. If action is not taken against the offender, the complainant becomes angry and blames the police for inaction. Pranks, misdemeanours and criminality get confused in our highly organised society. Legislation affects every aspect of life and impinges more and more on personal freedom. The people who have to enforce these laws are inevitably often seen as the 'instruments of oppression'. Indeed, if laws were fully enforced, the work of the police would really become impossible, everyone would have something to complain about, and law and order would certainly break down. The motorist who has been fined for a parking offence and who then has his house broken into, tends to see these events as a sign of police inefficiency—the police have their priorities wrong. The suggestion that ordinary citizens have a responsibility for the functioning of the law is regarded as unacceptable. We all tend to forget that the police are our agents and must perform the task for which we pay them—administering the law.

One aspect of police activity which contributes to tension between police and public is the use of police discretion. Decisions to take action against offenders are made by the police in the first stage; some decisions are clear cut and there is no choice on what must be done. Many times, because of the tremendous amount of trivial legislation, decisions have to be made as to whether a simple verbal warning by the police will be adequate, or more serious action is needed. Many petty offences are constantly ignored, indeed are probably forgotten. Without this, life would be intolerable for everyone. Police discretion in the case of minor offences is influenced by a multitude of factors, quite apart from the actual legality of the situation. Everyone has their own perception of when the police should take action. Every police officer will have his own perception of when he should act and how. The police force is largely a reactive force and their reaction will, in some degree, depend on outside pressure. Pressure may come from local communities, and the effectiveness of this pressure will depend on what sort of area is involved. Residents in deprived urban areas may find their pressure is less effective than residents in middle-class suburbs. Pressure from the media may influence action. The press are fond of making certain offences fashionable and will be quick to draw attention to any police failure to act. Political pressure is always there; a powerful politician will influence policing in his area, and will be quick to jump on the law and order bandwagon using local problems to enhance his power. During the era of gang problems in a Scottish city, a local politician made strong complaints about groups of youngsters wandering around his home area. Extra patrols were put on. One Sunday evening a group of lads from a hostel were returning from church with the hostel staff. They turned a street corner ahead of the staff; when the staff came round the corner they found the boys lined up against a wall, surrounded by a group of policemen. Such incidents create tension between police and the young who find it hard to understand—or who are unwilling to try to understand—the reasons for the police action.

Police discretion is also affected by the perceptions of the divisional commander, by the local beat officer and, less directly, the chief constable. The important influence of the divisional commander is borne out by a study of juvenile offending in a Scottish city division over a ten-year period. The pattern of offences showed regular changes—with a differing peak offence tending to go in cycles. It was possible to date almost exactly the changes of divisional commander by these 'crime waves'. For example, one commander was very tough on group disorder, another on football in the street, another on weapon carrying, and so on. Whatever offence was regarded as one to be dealt with, became the immediate concern of all patrols in the area; the traditional response that a show of strength will stamp out the problem. This often works, particularly with parking offences, speeding and other such misdemeanours but the effect is almost always transitory. Judging from the juvenile crime figures mentioned, the effect there was also very transitory. Because of the discretionary power of the police, it is inevitable that many decisions on action will raise dissension in some sections of the community and create tensions. It is important that police discretion is used widely and is explained clearly to those concerned, and that the community appreciates the pressures put on the police from various sources, pressures that force action.

The increasing influence of the media has added to the pressures put on the police and can exacerbate difficult situations. Crime is a tempting subject for the Press; it sells newspapers, it makes people switch on their TVs. Because so few people have direct contact with crime and violence or even with the police, opinions are formed from indirect and frequently distorted evidence, as supplied by the media. The favourite topics are invariably those which involve violent confrontations or situations—group disorders, industrial disputes, big robberies, football hooliganism, processions and murder—so it is not surprising if the ordinary citizen tends to get rather a distorted idea of what is happening around him. As far as the police are concerned, stories of police brutality, mishandling and harassment make much more interesting reading than the ordinary, rather dull, daily police activity. If there is a big demonstration the press will feature either a large policeman putting the boot into a demonstrator or the policeman getting the boot himself, depending on what the paper is and what the public mood demands. In both cases, no one will know what leads up to the actual incident, it will be seen out of context and, whichever side is featured, the reported story will aggravate bad feelings somewhere. Dealing with the media is a skill that the police are learning. The times when helpful co-operation has benefited a police investigation are numerous—but the problem of how to report crime and violence has not been thought out and few would argue that the present approach is ideal. Press reporting can reinforce crime fashions by influencing both offenders and the forces of law and order.

One of the interesting contrasts in police-public attitudes, and one which is probably partly influenced by the media, is the difference between what the public think that police work entails, what the police consider to be their work, and the way in which the public use the police and the police respond. Most policeman say that their job is to lock up villains and that is the job that they do. Many members of the public have the idea that the police spend their time persecuting them, particularly if they are motorists! In fact, studies of the use of police time made by analysing calls to police stations in both the UK and the USA show that only around 20-30 per cent of the calls were strictly law enforcement and between 50 and 70 per cent were 'service' type calls, concerned with health, domestic problems, errands and property. In many of these calls, the police fulfil a semi-social work type of role. In spite of criticisms and complaints on both sides, the public turn to the police in a multitude of emergency situations and the police readily respond to these demands. This is what police work is about but it is also the side of police work for which there is little or no training. In an emergency the policeman may have to be a doctor, plumber, social worker, etc. and, when one considers that many policemen will be in their early twenties, lacking a wide experience of life, the fact that most policemen respond adequately to so many different demands is surprising. This side of policing tends to be forgotten, neglected or devalued and denied. It is, however, probably a side that gives the average beat officer the most satisfaction, although he may deny this and insist that the thing he enjoys most is 'locking up villians'.

As society becomes increasingly urbanised and the police are confined more and more to being a reactive service, playing a 'fire brigade role', functioning from their cars, so the police will become very dependent on public co-operation and will need new methods for getting closer to the public. The maintenance of law and order is far more complicated than simply catching offenders. Even this becomes more difficult in an anonymous society. Limited manpower resources reduce the chances of crime being detected and prevented without considerable public support and co-operation. To police the community without this co-operation and support, as a sort of army of occupation, will limit the effectiveness of the police and reduce their chances of ever really coming to grips with the problem of crime. In many deprived areas of our cities, the crime rate is alarmingly high and the 'clear-up rate' (i.e. the number of offenders caught and charged) alarmingly low. It is often in just these areas that the relationship between police and public is particularly poor. The police presence may be limited to a quick drive through by a panda car and there is little or no chance of making any real contact with the local population. In one such area in the west of Scotland, it was decided to open a local police office and restore the best officers. This led to improvement not only of relationships between police and the local community but also in the involvement of other services. In addition, there was a dramatic rise in the 'clear-up rate' for crimes committed in the area. This is a preventive measure which requires a large allocation of police resources. It is generally accepted by all forces as a priority to get men back on the street.

In really serious crime the police are able to be effective because of the enormous input of resources, but even here they need public support for information which will give them the leads they often need. In petty crime—minor thefts, housebreakings, car theft, vandalism—the police are heavily dependent on the public. It is unlikely that the policeman will witness these offences but it is very likely that members of the public will chance on such incidents. The only way of dealing with many of these petty offences is by catching the offender in the act and the chances of doing this are remote without the co-operation of local people. Too often the people who are most indignant about vandalism in their area and are loud in demanding that 'the police should do something about it', are themselves slow to report suspicious incidents. Without local information, without the assistance of the eyes and ears of the local people, the ability of the police to clear up many of these offences is very limited. In cases of serious threats to life and property, police resources will be poured into an area but to take such action to deal with minor incidents would be absurdly extravagant.

How does one have an impact on crime? Fear of punishment is the great deterrent, or so many believe, and certainly the police support this view. Unfortunately, many offenders do not expect to be caught or stop to think that they may be. A great deal of offending, particularly the day-to-day nuisance offending, is impulsive, unplanned, a chance occurrence, a seized opportunity, a response to a mood and, as such, is not likely to be deterred. The prevention of crime in modern society is much more complicated and sophisticated than simple deterrence through tough sentencing. In *The Policeman in the Community* (1964), Michael Banton says

> In today's circumstances new methods are needed to inculcate social norms; there will have to be greater reliance upon internal controls deriving from early socialisation and schooling and less reliance upon external controls such as punishment. Some social institutions will have to be overhauled to encourage citizen participation to a greater extent than at present.

Many police forces are beginning to realise just this fact and to rethink their attitude towards the community. It is becoming increasingly accepted that crime prevention is not a role that the police can fulfil in isolation. Even straight physical crime prevention is dependent for its success on co-operation from the community. The police can put forward ideas but it is the public who must make these ideas work. If the public responded fully to police advice on the use of locks, protection of property, storage of goods etc., the incidence of such crimes as theft, breaking and entering and robbery would certainly be reduced. Similarly, public awareness of forms of offending combined with a readiness to report suspicious behaviour, would have an impact on crime figures.

Unfortunately, some procedures suggested by the police are used thoughtlessly, inefficiently or carelessly by the public and create as many problems as they might solve. For example, the use of burglar alarms—false alarm calls are a constant drain on police time and very often a result of carelessness or neglect. Shoplifting, which at the moment is a growth industry, is aggravated by methods of displaying goods. Provoking impulse buying may also provoke impulse shoplifting. Locking cars and front doors, shutting windows, remembering to cancel papers and milk when going on holiday, taking care in the storage of money, are all areas where the public are extraordinarily negligent, and therefore fail to play their part in the prevention of crime. If everyone understood and cooperated in all these ways, crime would decrease. All the technology in the world is useless if the human factor fails. However skilful and diligent the police may be, they are helpless without public support. Of course, if the public feel alienated from the police, if there is a communication gap between the police and the community, then support of any kind will be less than complete and any efforts the police make will be undermined. Imposing law and order on an alienated community is a losing battle. This happens in some urban areas—it could happen in all urban areas if the gap between police and community continues to widen; if the police fail to accept that they cannot be successful without the goodwill of the public and the public fail to accept that their role in supporting the police is vital.

Some people believe that all that is needed is increased police efficiency and manpower and that, given this, maintaining law and order would present no problems. Increased efficiency and more men on the streets are important, but alone they will have small effect. There is little doubt that the shortage of manpower has not helped police-public relations. With less men on the ground there is less time for spending with the public—more men on the streets would help public relations, but alone would not solve the problem. Research has proved the firmly held belief that the mere fact of a policeman standing on the street, or a police car parked on a motorway, has an impact on the level of offending. A Home Office Research Project showed that one policeman in uniform had about a 20-30 per cent preventive effect. Two policemen did not double this percentage. The real impact is when the local community get to know, accept and understand their local policemen—not an easy task in these days of greater centralisation which removes the local flavour from the service.

The realisation of the importance of public support has led the police to develop their crime prevention efforts in two directions. First, physical crime prevention has been developed and crime prevention panels, consisting of members of the public, have been set up all over the country. These panels consist of businessmen, insurance companies and ordinary members of the public who meet regularly and discuss various problems of security. The idea sounds a good one but in fact it seems to have mixed benefits as there is little that these panels can do effectively and most of their time is spent talking. Of course, the exchange of ideas is always useful and crime prevention panels have become very sophisticated in their ideas for mechanical crime prevention, although rather less co-operative when individual members find their business interests threatened. There is also a tendency for crime prevention panels to demand action from the police and to fail to see that they themselves should contribute more. There is often a lot of talk about community action but little real action is taken. The vague remit given to panels and the absence of any real, identifiable role inevitably causes frustration which, in turn, leads to disinterest and a tendency to throw everything back to the police. There is a lot that crime prevention panels could do in educative terms if the groups were carefully selected from people with some skill to contribute and if the police produced some ideas for the panels. Perhaps widening the role of the panels so as not to be just a police responsibility, but rather a local authority responsibility, general to all local authority departments, would produce more ideas. Crime prevention is much more than police work. Education, social work, planning and architecture all have a part to play.

The second aspect of crime prevention which the police are increasingly developing is social crime prevention. This aspect of crime prevention is much more controversial and is only gradually gaining acceptance by police forces in Britain. The aim of social crime prevention is to get closer to the community and stimulate community response. In order to do this, projects are mounted in deprived areas and various clubs and activities are organised for the young and police officers. In some forces, young offenders are supervised by policemen and support is given to parents who seek help. This form of crime prevention can be compared with the development of preventive medicine and the role of the doctor. Initially, doctors simply treated and cured disease; in modern medicine the most important role for the doctor is the prevention of disease. This is done by education, inoculation and various preventive treatments, and the impact on the health of the community has been enormous; TB and many childhood ailments have disappeared, people live longer and are healthier than ever before. It would be optimistic to believe that any form of crime prevention could have the same effect on crime but there is no reason why it should not have some impact. Early preventive medicine was regarded with profound suspicion by many eminent doctors. Indeed, some preventive procedures are still viewed with doubt, such as the recent hostility to whooping cough vaccine. If this happens in a scientific discipline such as medicine, how much more so is it likely to happen in the far vaguer field of social crime prevention.

It is particularly important that the police establish good relationships with the young for it is with this group of the community that they need to develop their preventive ideas. The problem is that establishing good communication with the young is not easy. It is a skill that not everyone has, although it can be improved with training and practice. This suggests that a specialist approach is needed to deal with this problem. This was recognised in an address given by Sir Joseph Simpson, then Commissioner of the Metropolitan Police, to the Annual General Meeting of the Institute for the Study and Treatment of Delinquency in November 1967.[1] Sir Joseph pointed out that the role of the police in preventing and treating juvenile delinquency has never been precisely defined and had been subject to change over the years. There was a feeling in the police service that failure to take the young offender to court on the occasion of his first offence might mean a chance lost for preventing the youngster developing a criminal career. Because of their experience as law enforcement officers, the average policeman tends to be rather cynical and reactionary about the treatment and prevention of juvenile delinquency. Sir Joseph did not see treatment as a role for the police, but he did emphasise the need for specialist officers whose role should be to act as a bridge between various welfare agencies, the community and the police service as a whole. Other countries recognised the need for a specialist police service and Sir Joseph expressed the hope that such a specialist role might be developed in Britain.

Now, ten years on, it seems as though Sir Joseph's wish may be realised as the police are gradually coming to accept that there is more to curing crime than locking up villains. However, the problems and rewards of the social crime prevention approach are such that the idea is not easy to sell to the traditional policeman who has a tough urban area to handle. It sounds too much like 'going soft' and, if the police are seen to be going soft, they fear the situation may really get out of hand. Attitudes like this die hard and as long as they are around, social crime prevention will be an uphill task. It is difficult enough to get through the hostility shown by the public. It is much tougher to get through the hostility and suspicion of the police themselves. It is being done, and very successfully, in many parts of the UK. There is good reason for hoping that the police may win this very tough battle.

Notes

1. J. Simpson, 'The Police and Juvenile Delinquency', *British Journal of Criminology* (1968), vol. 8, p. 119.

2 THE POLICE AND THE JUVENILE OFFENDER

The basis of social crime prevention with young offenders is the police caution, known as a warning in Scotland where, under Scots law, a caution has a different meaning. Since the early 1900s some police forces have used warnings for juvenile offenders, administered by senior, uniformed officers, in circumstances where the offender admitted his guilt, the police were satisfied that they had a case and the complainant did not insist on prosecution. The use of the caution varied from Force to Force and the decision to adopt the system depended on the attitude of the chief constable and senior officers. Some police forces never used the warning, some used it rarely. Glasgow City Police operated a system of formal warning from 1905; juvenile offenders and their parents were invited to attend a 'Superintendent's Court' where the warning was given.

A report on police warnings by the Scottish Advisory Council for the Rehabilitation of the Offender, in February 1945, indicated some reservations regarding the use of the police warning. These reservations were echoed by chief constables from all parts of the country and were very typical of the reservations which always seem to be voiced when new procedures are inaugurated, particularly when the procedures involve the diverting of offenders from traditional systems and can be interpreted as the offender 'getting away with it'. The main objections expressed were:

1. that there was no statutory authority for the warning or caution;
2. that the police might be accused of exceeding their powers;
3. that background information was not available and so the case might not be handled adequately;
4. that the warning was informal and so could not be referred to in any subsequent case.

In spite of the reservations, the Advisory Council, backed by the Secretary of State, recommended the adoption of the warning system by the Scottish police—a recommendation that was accepted by most of the 48 forces. The Scottish Advisory Council emphasised that the warning was in no way a court procedure; it could only be used if there was proof of guilt; it should only be used for first offenders and the relevant prosecuting authority, in Scotland the Procurator Fiscal, should be consulted in cases about which there was some doubt; that children brought to the police station for warning should have no contact with the formal business of the charge room or any court and that children dealt with in this way should not be included in criminal statistics.

These recommendations dealt with the overt fears and objections expressed by the police but they did not touch on what was probably the more important and basic anxiety, particularly for the average cop on the beat, the feeling that young offenders were 'getting away with it' and that the police were wasting their time trying to catch them. This feeling frequently pervades police thinking on experiments that fall within the area of social crime prevention. To the average policeman crime prevention is catching and locking up offenders; punishment and retribution must follow offending or crime will get out of hand. Crime prevention that involves bolts and burglar alarms is understandable but crime prevention that involves the diversion of young offenders outside of the criminal justice system is hard to accept. It is natural that policemen should feel thus for they are in at the start of many nasty and disturbing incidents involving young offenders; the policeman sees the misery caused by the anti-social actions of some youngsters and his natural reaction is that such behaviour should be punished; failure to punish is seen as an encouragement to further anti-social behaviour. In fact, a police warning at an early stage creams off cases which would not be dealt with at all under the juvenile justice system. These are cases in which no action would be taken.

Policemen tend to feel that the persistent offender continues with his offending because he has never been adequately punished. As one police officer commented; 'If a young person is caught thieving that means that he has a bad bit in him and the only way to deal with that bad bit is by punishment. Punishment will deter the youngster and do something about the bad bit'. It would be foolish to argue that no youngster has a 'bad bit', that they do not sometimes need a tough line. What tends to be overlooked is that minor anti-social behaviour is part of growing up. Most people have been involved in such behaviour at some time in their lives—apple scrumping, petty theft, minor vandalism—we have all done it at some time. Most people grow out of it quickly, some because they were caught and deterred by parental discipline, some because they were not caught. A police warning can sometimes reinforce parental discipline, sometimes take its place and have the desired effect in preventing further offending. To invoke the whole majesty of the law in cases that are very petty or in isolated occurrences is to make the law look foolish. Indeed, such proceedings may have a damaging effect and give the child offender a thrill of importance as the centre of attention, a real tough guy. In addition, if the youngster continues his offending, the effect of the court or panel will be diminished and the child's anti-social tendencies may be aggravated rather than deterred. The level of response to a child's offending is important. Over reaction can cause as much harm as under reaction. Children take time to learn the abstract sense of right and wrong, they may know that they will get into trouble if they behave in a certain way but abstract values develop as they mature into adults. Instilling these values is important and if youngsters are labelled as 'criminal', 'evil', 'useless scum', because they have committed minor misdemeanours which they know that most of their friends do anyway, they will start to believe that they are evil and should be 'put away' or they will feel unfairly treated. Either way, they may well respond by further offending. A policeman is in the front line and can have considerable influence on youthful misbehaviour. It is important for him to discriminate between the average childish misdemeanour and the really anti-social offender, not an easy task in any situation. Over reaction to childish misdeeds limits the options for more serious misbehaviour.

During the early 1960s the value of attempting to keep juvenile offenders out of the criminal justice system became increasingly accepted, but it was not until the Children and Young Persons Act (1969) was passed that the police in England were given statutory authority for cautioning juvenile offenders as an alternative to taking them to court. The police were stimulated into action by the impending Act and between 1968 and 1974 (the Act came into force in 1971) cautions increased from 33,700 to 101,235. This upsurge of cautioning in England had a diversionary effect as far as court proceedings were concerned. In spite of a rise in juvenile offending between 1968 and 1973 there was a reduction of approximately 6,000 children appearing in court. However, the impact as far as offending was concerned would appear to be inflationary in that the areas where cautioning was most frequently used were also areas where juvenile offending showed the greatest increase. This may be due to the fact that many unofficial street warnings now became more official station cautions, and shops and other premises that had previously been reluctant to call in the police when juveniles were caught committing petty thefts, now became more ready to do so. Indeed, in Liverpool when the juvenile liaison scheme was being planned, it was discovered that many children caught pilfering were not reported to the police because the shops could not provide staff to attend court. This attitude is almost certainly typical of many areas.

The effectiveness of the caution as a deterrent to further offending by the juvenile is difficult to assess. Most police forces quote figures such as 80 per cent of those cautioned do not reoffend. The reliability of such figures is open to doubt as records of cautions tend to be scrappy and their accuracy questionable. A study of police cautioning compared with juvenile liaison by Gordon Rose and R.A. Hamilton[1] suggested that the success rate for cautioning was around 60-70 per cent. This study also makes the point that there was no evidence at all that juvenile liaison supervision had any impact on recidivism, either during or after supervision. 'The rate would have been very similar if they had all been cautioned only.'

One wonders if cautions given formally in the police station are really any more effective than the personal warnings given on the street every day by police officers. Of course, the set up of the station warning is given enough attention to have some impact on the impressionable, minimally delinquent child who is not used to being in such places. The situation of the formal warning gives a conflicting impression. The appearance of the superintendent in full uniform is guaranteed to impress the inexperienced offender. After attending several warnings, I am left with the impression that such young offenders are rare. I noted several 12-13-year-olds who were obviously very sophisticated in their relationship with the police and were able to take the whole event in their stride, glowering back at the superintendent. They were used to being told off by policemen and knew all they had to do was endure a telling-off. The parents seemed more shaken by the proceedings than the youngsters, fear and shame showing vividly on their faces. Younger children seemed to be more fearful, but one felt that they probably heard little of what was said, and understoood less. Occasionally a parent would become truculent, insisting that their child was being victimised by the police. At least one father was rather the worse for drink, no doubt taken to build up his courage. All the parents made fervent promises regarding the future behaviour of their children and were full of assurances of more careful supervision in the future. Several mothers wept although only a minority of the children seemed remotely distressed.

In spite of the obvious effort put into the warning situation, the impression given was that, on the whole, few of the police officers concerned really managed to communicate with the youngsters. This failure is not peculiar to the police, for many other professionals dealing with the young lack the skill to communicate with those they seek to help. If a child's attention is not caught by the first few words spoken, if he feels 'just another lecture', what is said will have little impact. Thought and training need to be given for each occasion. No doubt the impact of a caution is more than just what is said. It is the cumulative effect of the whole visit to the police station on the child and the parents. If, in addition, the warning officer can achieve some level of communication with the child it may enhance the preventive effect and establish more positive attitudes to the police in the young. It would seem that the warning is a situation where the use of specially trained officers is of great importance.

Juvenile liaison schemes are a development of the cautioning system and involve the use of specially selected, and sometimes specially trained, officers. The first attempt at such a specialist police service was set up in Liverpool in 1949. This was an experimental scheme established by Liverpool City Police in response to the escalation in juvenile offending and the realisation that many petty offenders were not being reported to the police and were drifting into more serious crime. In a foreword to a booklet on the scheme *The Police and the Children*,[2] the Chief Constable defined how he saw the scheme functioning:

> One of the primary functions of the police is the prevention as well as the detection of crime and by the very nature of our duties and responsibilities we are ideally situated to learn of potential delinquents at an early stage and take immediate action to prevent them developing criminal tendencies.

He went on to describe the scheme as 'filling the gap' between the welfare services and the community problem of young offenders. Filling, and bridging, this gap is probably one of the most important roles in any preventive policing experiment.

This pilot project in Liverpool was so successful that in 1952 a Juvenile Liaison Department was established as part of the Crime

Prevention Branch of Liverpool City Police. In 1954 the merits of juvenile liaison were considered by the Advisory Council on the Treatment of Offenders in England and Wales and by the Association of Chief Police Officers. The Home Office then circulated details of the scheme to police forces all over the country, leaving it to chief constables to decide whether such a scheme was appropriate for their area. In 1960 the whole concept of juvenile liaison received a setback when the Ingleby Committee responded negatively to the ideas. They commended both the aims and achievements of juvenile liaison schemes but did not recommend the general adoption of such schemes as they considered the role of a police officer was incompatible with the demands of the role of a juvenile liaison officer. We will return to this problem later.

In 1956 the first juvenile liaison officers were appointed in Scotland by the Chief Constable of Greenock, David Gray. This project was initiated as part of a crime prevention exercise which included the usual physical crime prevention and also close co-operation with local government departments in rehabilitating deprived housing areas in the town and developing a strong police interest in organising youth clubs and recreational activities.[3] The juvenile liaison officers became involved not only in supervising offenders but also in going to the schools, participating in camping trips for the young and generally establishing closer relationships with the local community. This development of the police role in the community was the start, albeit a very gradual one, of a whole new area of police activity in Scotland.

In 1964 the Kilbrandon Committee, the Scottish equivalent of the Ingleby Committee, came out positively in favour of juvenile liaison and commended it as a progressive police function. The provision was added that the difference of role between police liaison officers and social workers should be clearly defined on paper. However, in their evidence to the Kilbrandon Committee the Association of Chief Police Officers (Scotland) firmly rejected the idea of juvenile liaison. Four Scottish chief constables in favour of the idea presented a separate memorandum to the Committee in 1963.

The one and only juvenile liaison scheme in London was established at West Ham in 1961 and by 1969 there were 17 such schemes in England and Wales and 8 in Scotland. Most of the schemes followed the pattern set by the Liverpool projects. Two categories of children were defined as being appropriate for supervision: firstly, children who had committed an offence but had not come to the attention of the police before; secondly, children who had not committed an offence but had been brought to the notice of the police by their parents, teachers or other police officers for playing truant, being unruly, staying out at night or being otherwise at risk. The Scottish chief constables who were in favour of juvenile liaison laid out clear guidelines regarding the conditions necessary for admission to the scheme. These were to be:

1. First offenders who admitted an offence which was not of a serious nature and were warned by a senior officer, and for whom it was thought supervision might be useful.
2. Children who steal from their own homes and persist in so doing in spite of parental efforts to prevent it.
3. Children who have been caught stealing but the owner of the stolen property insists on no court action.
4. Children whose conduct is not yet criminal but shows every likelihood of becoming so. Examples of such children are those who frequently run away from home, persistently stay out late at night against the wishes of their parents, or who are keeping bad company.
5. Children under the age of criminal responsibility who are found committing crimes or offences.

The qualification for admission to the schemes were:

1. The offender must be a child or young person, i.e. under 17 years old.
2. The crime or offence must be of a minor nature.
3. The crime or offence must be admitted by the child and parents.
4. The parents must agree to co-operate.

The procedure followed for dealing with young offenders by juvenile liaison was for the child to receive a verbal warning from a senior officer in uniform. Thereafter, subject to the agreement of the parents, the juvenile liaison officer followed up the offender by keeping in touch with the youngster, enlisting the co-operation of his family, school, youth club and, if necessary, the social services. In a way, the role taken by the juvenile liaison officer resembled that of the 'village bobby', an informal, controlling approach—'an attempt to reproduce in the more congested and anonymous conditions of an urban area a liaison which operates without formal contrivance in a village'.[4]

The immediate effect in most areas was a reduction in the numbers of juveniles appearing in the juvenile court. In Greenock between the years 1956 and 1959 the number of juveniles appearing before the courts reduced from 517 to 265. The types of cases taken on were theft, truancy, running away from home and minor house-breaking. In Liverpool the length of supervision was six months, in West Ham the length tended to be six to nine months but there were variations ranging from one week to three years. In Scotland the average length was nine months, but again there was considerable variation. John Mack suggested that perhaps long periods of super-vision were unwise because it meant that the families had to stagger along without specialist help for too long a period. He suggested that juvenile liaison schemes should always consider seeking expert advice and help from other services.

It is with potential offenders that the police, through their spe-cialist officers, can render the most effective crime prevention role. It is the police who are most likely to become aware of a child's potentially anti-social behaviour. This may be through observations of uniformed officers, it may be through a request for help from the parents or from some other source, such as the school. The interven-tion of a juvenile liaison officer at this stage can give parents support and help youngsters to change their habits. In addition, by forming positive and helpful relationships with such youngsters, the police officer can bridge the gap that so often exists between families and the police. It is interesting to note in this context that in Liverpool the numbers of potential offenders, informally referred, gradually increased until 1962 when they accounted for one-third of cases referred to the Department.

Just how successful were these early juvenile liaison experiments? A study by Gordon Rose and R.A. Hamilton of the Blackburn and Manchester experiments found that the children supervised did no better than those who were cautioned.[5] The authors go on to indicate that they do not consider this finding to mean that the juvenile liaison officers had failed to help the children they had supervised or that they were, in any way, inefficient; rather that the results were related to the population served where recidivism was likely to be high anyway. They go on to suggest that the better understanding of the police role and the good relationships established with other agencies with whom the juvenile liaison officers had contact, were as important as the effect on the children supervised, as these agencies developed a more positive view of the police. It is relevant to comment here on a film made of the Blackburn Police juvenile liaison officers at work. This film gave a disturbing view of how these juvenile liaison officers functioned. Supervision of the young offenders seemed to involve a mixture of bullying and threats that might be expected to destroy any chance of these officers forming constructive relationships with the young they supervised. If this approach were general among juvenile liaison officers in other areas, and I know that this is not the case, juvenile liaison schemes would achieve nothing.

A Home Office Research Unit study[6] of the West Ham juvenile liaison scheme reached similar conclusions to those reached by Rose and Hamilton. The Home Office study went further by suggesting that the juvenile liaison officers made contact with many children who did not come to the attention of other agencies, and they were able to refer some of the more seriously disturbed children to other agencies for more specialised help. Had it not been for the intervention of the police, these children might never have received specialist help. The assessment of the Liverpool experiment by the police suggests a higher success rate than in other areas. This study also lays great stress on the positive effects on other agencies of the juvenile liaison experiment. Closer relationships and a deeper understanding developed between police and both social work agencies and schools.

As these studies demonstrate, no one has attempted to evaluate juvenile liaison schemes solely in terms of the recidivism rate of the young offenders supervised. The objectives of juvenile liaison schemes are much wider and the hopes of what they may achieve are far greater than individual successes. Through juvenile liaison the police started to find their way back into the community and the community began to develop a more realistic understanding of the police. The establishment of such relationships can only be constructive and have a positive impact on the young in the community.

If the general impact of juvenile liaison on the community was positive, what was the impact on the individual officers appointed to carry out these duties? They faced many problems. There was hostility both from within the police and from outside. Probation officers saw the juvenile liaison officer as a threat to them, an attempt by untrained police officers to undertake a social work role for which they were untrained. On the police side the juvenile liaison officer was seen as a pseudo-social worker, no longer a 'real policeman'. Fulfilling a new and difficult role in a service where there is hostility on all sides is a difficult and testing job for anyone. In a study of juvenile liaison,[7] Maureen Cain points out that hostility to juvenile liaison in the police service was inevitable, as was the role conflict which most juvenile liaison officers experienced. The reason for this is that the only real measure of the success a policeman has is the 'clear-up rate', the number of offenders caught and taken to court. The aim of operational policing is to search, chase, capture and bring to court. The juvenile liaison officer, on the other hand, has the duty to keep his charges out of court. The whole aim of his work is crime prevention and, as such, is not the most popular role among the police. It must be said that there is increasing realisation that preventive policing, like preventive medicine, is of crucial importance. Such understanding percolates slowly through the police service and was rare in the early days of juvenile liaison schemes. An additional problem for the juvenile liaison officer was that he had to deal with potential offenders—children who had committed no offence but were considered to be at risk. Such cases were not recorded in police statistics, could not be used to boost the 'clear-up rate' and were, in effect, work that was 'lost'. As such, it would not be popular with divisional commanders.

Resolving the personal role conflict was difficult for many juvenile liaison officers. Reconciling the traditional law and order role of the police with the new social service role of the juvenile liaison officer required maturity. Some officers tended to over react and become excessively involved in their cases. Others carried on in the same way as before sometimes taking their juvenile liaison status as a licence to extend their pressure on the young (notably in Blackburn!). The majority acquired the skill of treading the narrow path between over involvement and non-involvement, giving the young offenders a chance to make what may well be their first real contact with authority. A senior officer, recalling his time as a juvenile liaison officer, said he did not find it difficult to move from the CID to juvenile liaison as he found his experience as a detective enabled him to talk to young people. The problem arose when he left the juvenile liaison department and returned to operational policing. He found that the 'edge' had been taken off him because he had lost contact with 'real' offenders. He found that in time this 'edge' returned and he now felt that his experience in juvenile liaison had, in fact, made him a better policeman by broadening his outlook. It was, he said, a very narrow and difficult path that he discovered he had to tread as a juvenile liaison officer. On the one hand, he had to gain the confidence of the young offenders and help them to change their ways; on the other, he had to keep in mind the fact that he was a police officer, and there were times when he had to take action to deal more punitively with some youngsters that he was supervising. He was always aware that, as a police officer, he could never connive at any form of anti-social behaviour.

In 1974 the Glasgow City Police decided to try a juvenile liaison scheme using unit beat officers for supervisers. This scheme was initiated in a small sub-division which covered a post-war housing estate. The officers who were doing the supervision were given a two-day training, although, because of changes in personnel, many of those concerned missed the training sessions. After the scheme had been in operation for a year, the Chief Constable asked me to assess it. The Divisional and sub-Divisional Commanders were interviewed, as were the two Sergeants responsible for the area and all the supervising PCs. In addition, a sample of families whose children had received supervision under the scheme were interviewed in their homes. The supervision given by the PCs was very limited. Only a few interviews were involved but as the supervising officers were the local PCs, they were able to have a certain amount of informal contact with their charges in a way that is not usually possible for a specialist juvenile liaison officer. They were also aware of local problems and how these affected their particular youngsters.

During the period of the project there had been a change of both Divisional and sub-Divisional Commander. Both new senior officers were considerably less enthusiastic about the scheme than the original officers. Indeed, one was extremely hostile to the whole idea, considering that supervision of young offenders was not a job for policemen and certainly not for his beat officers. This caused problems for the PCs who were uncertain as to how much attention they should give to their supervising role. Before interviewing the PCs, I was told by the Divisional Commander that all of them were very hostile to the scheme and considered it a waste of time. The sub-Divisional Commander expressed the same view. The Sergeant in charge of the supervising PCs did not approve of the scheme but had put a lot of energy into making it work because that was what the Chief Constable wanted. In fact, this officer rather changed his view after visiting all the families to get their agreement for me to visit and discuss the supervision. He found that most of the families were very positive about the police involvement and he felt that the scheme had done the police image a lot of good. He did add, however, that he was still not convinced that this was a role for police officers!

When interviewed individually, the PCs who had done the supervising showed a wide range of views about the scheme. Most said that they had been hostile when they heard about the project, but only two officers of the 15 interviewed said that they had not changed this view after having been involved for a year. As these two officers had the busiest sections in the area and were already overworked, their hostility was not surprising. Their reaction was 'one more burden for the police who have to take over because social workers can't do their job properly'.

The most difficult problem for the supervising PCs was resolving the conflict between their 'law and order' and 'social service' roles. One officer described how bad he felt when he had had to charge a lad who he had been supervising. He felt that he had failed and the child would feel he had been let down. Most of the PCs insisted that they would not hesitate to charge their youngsters should the need arise, but they felt this could be confusing for the children. This conflict is not unique to the police although perhaps it is more obvious. Probation officers and others involved in treatment of offenders have to resolve the problem of dealing with those of their clients who get involved in further offending. Treatment which involves conniving at further offences in order to keep the offender out of court is unlikely to achieve much in terms of changing patterns of anti-social behaviour. It takes a mature and experienced person to resolve this conflict satisfactorily, and training and experience are important in developing this skill. To expect the juvenile liaison officer who is minimally trained, or the ordinary PC who may have had no special training, to resolve this conflict instinctively, is asking a lot, particularly of the younger men.

The families interviewed were largely very positive about the supervision their children had been given. They had found the support of the police officer a help in their efforts to cope with their youngsters and their problems. One mother, who was widowed, complained that she thought the supervising officer had overdone the disciplinary approach with her son but admitted that she was inclined to be soft with the lad as he was all she had. Several parents said they would have preferred the police to have visited in plain clothes, finding the constant calls of uniformed officers embarrassing. In fact, the question of uniform had been discussed at the start of the project and it had been decided that all supervisory calls must be made in uniform, this being a condition of supervision. One father summed up the general attitude of the families saying 'I was kind of surprised that the police could be so helpful. They took a real interest in the lad. I reckon it was good for him.'

One interesting aspect of this project was the difference of views expressed by the police officers when seen individually from the views given as a group and described by their divisional commander. Indeed, the commander regarded the results with some suspicion because they were so different to what he had expected. In fact, the project illustrates one of the problems policemen face. In a disciplined service, the junior officers are expected to enforce the law and display attitudes which are regarded as appropriate by their senior officers. It is the senior officer who recommends a man for promotion, it is the senior officer who comments on a man's record. On the whole the police are fairly representative of the community when taken as individuals. *En masse* they tend to reflect the attitude of their senior officers. It is unlikely that an individual policeman would resist the pressure of the group and his commander and frankly express what he thinks may be minority views. As one individual officer interviewed said:

With all these changes in commander and consequent changes in attitude, we really don't know where we are. Do we spend our time trying to lock more people up? Doing enquiries for the CID? Booking traffic offenders? Or do we concentrate our time on our supervision cases? All the bosses seem to have different ideas.

The ordinary PC does not have an easy path to tread and may have to suppress his own views in the interests of his career. It is this process that sometimes gives the community the idea that there is a 'police view' and 'police behaviour'. It is this process that makes the selection of senior officers such a vital and delicate matter.

This experimental project was not extended although in several parts of the Strathclyde Police area, PCs take on individual offenders for supervision. In other areas of England and Scotland home beat officers are involved in supervision but shortage of manpower limits the numbers that can get thus involved.

The question that must be asked now is whether juvenile liaison can be regarded as a legitimate role for the police? The Ingleby Committee thought not; many police officers of every rank, in forces that have juvenile liaison schemes and those that do not, are actively hostile to the whole idea. Acute differences of opinion between chief constables who supported juvenile liaison and those who did not were highlighted in Scotland by evidence given to the Kilbrandon Committee. The education, social work and welfare services were initially very hostile, although opinions tended to change once they had actually worked with juvenile liaison officers. The hostility of the senior police officers made life particularly difficult for juvenile liaison officers because, however enthusiastic the chief constable may be, it takes a very determined chief constable to ensure that all his divisional commanders are abiding by the spirit of his instructions. Divisional commanders hostile to juvenile liaison could undermine the juvenile liaison officer. In some cases, they went so far as to block promotion for these officers. We saw in the Glasgow City Police experiment how changes in divisional commander unsettled the supervising PCs, making them uncertain of how much attention they should give to the supervision. In spite of the hostility and the problems of their role, the juvenile liaison officers have generally achieved high ranks in the police and have shown themselves particularly able at comprehending the wider implications of law and order.

A favourite anti-juvenile liaison argument which is particularly prevalent at the present time is that, when resources are limited, should valuable police strength be diverted to a 'Social Work' role. If the police accept, and most do, that their main task is the prevention of crime, how can they object to prevention that is being attempted by positive means? Prevention that seeks to prevent the potential offender becoming the real offender, the minor offender from becoming the persistent offender, is as valid as the hardware of prevention, the burglar alarms and bolts which are rarely the object of hostility. Social crime prevention should be, in fact, more effective than physical crime prevention. The juvenile liaison officer may succeed in diverting a child from a criminal career, the burglar alarm is likely only to divert the offender to another, less well-protected property. In addition, the more the community, particularly the young in the community, get to know policemen as individuals who are concerned and sympathetic as well as controlling and disciplining, the more chance there will be of improving communication and co-operation between police and public. Policing in a democratic society is impossible without this co-operation. It is fair to say that the early juvenile liaison experiments started a process of bridging a gap that is slowly narrowing and gaining momentum.

Notes

1. 'Effects of a Juvenile Liaison Scheme', *British Journal of Criminology* (1970), vol. 10, no. 1

2. Liverpool City Police, 1964.

3. See Chapter 5.

4. Mack, J., 'Police Juvenile Liaison Schemes', *British Journal of Criminology* (April 1963).

5. 'Effects of a Juvenile Liaison Scheme', *British Journal of Criminology* (1970), vol. 10, no. 1.

6. Home Office Research Unit, *Report No. 8.*

7. Maureen Cain, 'Role Conflict Among Police Juvenile Liaison Officers', *British Journal of Criminology* (1968), vol. 8, no. 4.

3 THE POLICE AND THE NEW LEGISLATION

Police experimental schemes with juvenile offenders were given increased impetus by new legislation brought in during the 1960s. This new legislation developed as a result of official concern regarding the escalating problem of juvenile crime and the high level of child neglect and cruelty exposed by the evacuation of children during World War II. Evacuation schemes brought home to the public as well as the government just how widespread were poverty and deprivation among urban families. Many studies were undertaken and it became clear that action was necessary to deal with the increasing level of urban deprivation, problem families, poverty, child neglect and juvenile delinquency. There was—and still is—general ignorance regarding the causation of juvenile offending but its relationship to urban deprivation cannot be disputed. There was —and still is—no real certainty regarding the way to handle the juvenile offender. The only certainty was that the legislation that existed seemed to be having little impact and some believed that the system might be aggravating the problem. In addition there was dissatisfaction regarding the functioning of the social services—both from the point of view of their administrative structure and the overlapping of service given to those in need.

In Scotland the Kilbrandon Committee reported in 1964, proposing, among other things, new and radical ideas for dealing with the young offender. In 1966 there followed a White Paper—'Social Work and the Community'—which became the basis of a whole new system of juvenile justice in Scotland. In 1967 the Social Work (Scotland) Bill was presented to Parliament and it became law in July 1968.

As a result of this Act, all social services were integrated into a single department—the social work department—and became the responsibility of the local authority. This part of the Act became effective in 1969. The integration of all social services into one department was welcomed by most—too many anomalies had resulted from the lack of a co-ordinated service. However, the idea of a generic social worker was received with reservation by some, with dismay by others. The probation service disappeared—and with it many of the probation officers, leading to a reduction in service given to the courts. The dramatic increase in senior posts for social workers led to a draining of workers on the ground and every function of the social work department suffered—none more than the probation supervision. Because of the shortages, social work departments developed systems of priorities and, predictably, the service given to the offender and the courts was very low on the list. This had a considerable effect on the police force as well as the courts. Young probationers, caught reoffending, were found not only to have received no supervision, but frequently had no idea who their social worker was. In this situation some police forces decided to warn as many children as possible to ensure that at least some action was taken. Some children were warned more than once—a procedure that was generally agreed to be unsatisfactory. In all cases, the police invariably notified the social work department before warning a child so as to ensure that they did not trespass on a case that was already receiving attention. Another result of the lack of supervision was the increased use of institutional placements for young offenders and pressure on places in residential accommodation. As a result of the Act these institutions, formerly known as remand centres and approved schools, had now became assessment centres and List 'D' schools.

In 1971 Part III of the Act was implemented. This dealt with children in need of compulsory care and it introduced a revolutionary change in the approach to children in trouble. It removed all but a few categories of child offender from the criminal justice system and replaced juvenile courts with Children's Panels. These Panels are composed of ordinary members of the public who have been selected and trained by the local authority. The sittings of these Panels are known as Hearings and each Hearing must consist of three Panel members—a chairman and two others. One member of the Hearing must be female and one a male. The executive officials of the Children's Hearings are known as Reporters. This new profession which developed as part of the system has the specific responsibility of ensuring that the welfare of the child is always the paramount consideration in all decisions made by the Hearings. The Reporter makes the decision to bring the child to a Hearing; he decides whether further guidance is required for the Hearing from other experts and he must ensure that the Hearing is conducted in a manner which conforms to the legal requirements laid down by the Act. The weakness in the establishment of Reporters' Departments was that no specific professional requirements were demanded; in addition, no particular professional training was laid down. Reporters were appointed from a wide variety of professional backgrounds—social workers, policemen, lawyers, teachers and some new graduates. Lack of professional qualifications has led to variations in interpretation of the Reporter's role and some legal problems. A child can only be brought to a Hearing if he accepts the grounds of referral—frequently an offence. If he denies this, the case has to go to the Sheriff for proof. In addition, after the Hearing, if the family wish to appeal against the decision of the Hearing, the case again has to go to the Sheriff. Some Sheriffs objected to Reporters who had no legal training—and that applies to a large number—presenting cases in court. As a result of these objections by the Judiciary an amendment was passed to the Act, giving Reporters the right to appear in court. Such an answer is not entirely satisfactory as some legal expertise is important in such situations.

There are seven categories of juvenile offender that, on the instructions of the Lord Advocate, must still go to court. These include cases of murder, serious assault, robbery and fire raising, cases involving disqualification or forfeiture, a category referred at the discretion of the chief constable, and cases where an adult and child are involved together as it was considered unfair that they should be separated. In fact, the majority of such cases are split and the adult is dealt with in one way in Court and a different course is taken for the child at a Hearing. In addition, all custody cases have initially to be referred to the Procurator Fiscal. This is a procedure that sometimes leads to problems when, because of communication failures, parents turn up at the Sheriff Court only to find that their child is not appearing but has been referred to the Reporter.

The philosophy of the Hearing is that it should be as informal as possible and that the main consideration at all times must be the welfare of the child. Those usually present at a Hearing include the three Panel members, the Reporter, the child and his parents, and if the parents wish, a friend or legal adviser. In addition, a social worker, psychologist or other professional advisers may be present at the discretion of the Panel. The Hearings are conducted in accommodation specifically set aside for the purpose. Those involved sit round a table and every effort is made to involve the child and parents in discussion. No outsiders are admitted, except with the approval of the Hearing and the press are not admitted. Responsibility for order at the Hearing Centre rests with the Reporters, as does responsibility for conveying the child who is in custody to the Hearing. In exceptional cases the police may be requested for assistance. Apart from this, the only role the police have to play is to refer the child to the Reporter. Once a child is referred by the police, that is usually the end of the matter. Some police forces refer all child offenders to the Reporter and take back for warning those recommended by the Reporter. Minor cases, those where the evidence is doubtful and cases against children already under supervision for some other offence, are marked as 'no proceedings' by the Reporter. This procedure has been a source of irritation to the police in many areas, as it is considered that there are too many children committing offences about which nothing is done. Detectives particularly feel that they are often wasting their time catching the offenders. Reporters' Departments insist that the majority of 'no proceedings' are against children already under supervision or for offences that are so petty it is not worth bringing them to a Hearing. This is one of the reasons for the increase in police warnings. It is a cause for concern that children can commit petty offences—some of which may cause considerable distress to the victims—yet, after being caught by the police, nothing happens. Such children must develop a sense of immunity and be encouraged in their anti-social behaviour. It also does nothing for the cause of encouraging police co-operation.

The two sources of action open to the Hearings are: (i) supervision in the community or supervision in a residential institution; (ii) to discharge the case. The Hearing has no power to impose financial sanctions or to order reparation—although it is possible for the Hearing to get voluntary agreement from the child and his family to make some sort of reparation. Cases that come within the Lord Advocate's categories must be sent to a Hearing by the Sheriff for advice. All cases that go to a Hearing must be reviewed annually when the Hearing will decide whether the course of treatment should continue, be varied or be rescinded. Three months after a Hearing an offender can seek a review or a Hearing can be called at any time to vary the supervision requirements. Emergency Hearings can be called at any time if required.

It will be obvious that Part III of the Act resulted in a great change of role for the police. In order to define and clarify the situation a Working Party was set up by the Scottish Home and Health

Department before the implementation of the Act to look at police procedure resulting from it. The terms of reference for this Working Party were

> To review the procedure of the police in regard to children, including fingerprinting and the retention of records, in view of the changes which will arise from the implementation of Part III and Schedule 2 of the Social Work (Scotland) Act, 1968 and in the light of other relevant considerations, and to make recommendations.

The Working Party consisted of officials from the Scottish Home and Health Department, including HM Chief Inspector of Constabulary, the Social Work Services Group (the new Scottish Office department responsible for the integrated social work departments) and the Crown Office. A representative of the Chief Constables Association (Scotland) attended meetings as an observer and several organisations and individuals gave written and oral evidence to the Working Party. The final report dealt with co-operation between the police and social workers, police discretion, the police and the Children's Hearings, records, fingerprinting and photographing. The report pointed out that, if the Act was to work, the essential factor was that there should be mutual understanding and co-operation at all levels between the police and social work departments. This is the rock to which the Act is anchored or on which it may perish. Anxiety was expressed by members of the Working Party that chief constables who, quite properly, are preoccupied by problems of escalating crime, might be reluctant to accept the system set up by the Act. The chief constables responded by insisting that the ordinary policeman on the beat is well aware of the need of the juvenile offender for care and supervision—perhaps rather an optimistic statement at the time.

The Working Party discussed police discretion, the use of police warnings, juvenile liaison, responsibility for juvenile offenders and the particular role of the police. It was stipulated that once the police had reported a juvenile offender to the Reporter, police responsibility ceased; that children who had committed a serious offence should not be held in police cells for any longer than necessary, but should be transferred to the care of the social work department. The police should only be asked for assistance in transferring children in custody when the child is exceptionally unruly.

The keeping of records raised a lot of discussion; social work organisations and some individuals expressed concern at the idea that such records should be held by social work departments. The chief constables insisted that they must have immediate access to information regarding an offender's previous record of offending, and that these records must be available at any time of the day or night. This view was accepted by the majority of those involved. Fingerprinting and photographing offenders were two sensitive areas of discussion. The Working Party noted that the fingerprinting of children under the age of 14 is not permitted in England. Several organisations found the idea of fingerprinting children to be repugnant and irreconcilable with the philosophy of the Kilbrandon Report, which was the basis of the Act. In the view of the police, the need to detect offenders and bring them into care justified the finger-printing of children, although it was agreed that this should be done with discretion. This view was accepted by the majority of organisations. Photographing children was in a different category and the police considered that photographing juveniles was a waste of time as their appearance tended to change so quickly.

The report concluded by listing, in summary form, the recommended procedures for the police in the light of the principles discussed in the report. These were:

1. To establish in consultation with the social work department a general pattern of action in accordance with the circumstances of the area, including arrangements for the informal exchange of information regarding juvenile delinquency, and to promote liaison between the police and social workers at all levels.
2. To consider appointing specially selected officers to supervise the warning of juvenile offenders, juvenile liaison schemes, and to arrange for them to be trained in identifying those circumstances calling for professional social work assistance.
3. To bring to the notice of the social work department cases of incipient delinquency or children in need of care.
4. When an offence has been detected, to exercise discretion in considering whether to give an informal warning on the spot or a formal warning by a senior police officer, or whether to inform the Reporter or, in cases covered by the Lord Advocate's discretion, both the Procurator Fiscal and the Reporter.
5. If formal warning or juvenile liaison treatment is decided on, to inform the social work department.

6. The spirit in which the police handle suspected child offenders must reflect the objective which is to secure the correct method of treatment for the child, while taking whatever steps are necessary to identify the offender and secure adequate evidence in case the circumstances of the offence are not admitted.

7. In the case of an alleged offender aged between 16 and 18, to ascertain whether he is the subject of a supervision requirement and therefore subject to the Social Work Act procedures for children.

8. To take fingerprints primarily for the more serious offences involving older children, and only if they offer a substantial chance of detecting juvenile offenders who would otherwise escape the appropriate measures of care. Photographs should be taken in relatively few cases, e.g older juveniles. To arrange for parents to attend the police station if time allows, before fingerprints or photographs are taken.

9. A child should not be detained in custody unless he is suspected of committing a serious crime or is unusually recalcitrant. Arrangements should be made for the conveyance of a child who cannot be liberated to a suitable place of safety, in accordance with plans made in advance with the Reporter and the social work department. Every effort must be made to find accommodation other than a police station in which to detain such a child and, if detained in a police station, accommodation other than a cell should be arranged.

10. If police discretion is not to be exercised, to report the case to the Reporter or, in cases covered by the Lord Advocate's discretion, to both Procurator Fiscal and Reporter, and in addition, to make all relative background information available.

11. Formal police responsibility ceases thereafter unless the child is to be prosecuted or is unavoidably held in police custody, or police assistance is required in securing the attendance of the child at the Hearing or to maintain order at the Hearing.

12. To record the manner in which the reported case is disposed of (i.e. voluntary measures of care, compulsory measures of care, discharge by the Sheriff or findings of the court). Voluntary measures of care and discharge will not be centrally recorded, and compulsory measures of care will be carefully distinguished from court findings of guilt following prosecution. Records may be retained, but as at present, will not be disclosed except in the few categories where the public interest demands it.

13. Fingerprint records and photographs of children, if taken, will be destroyed except where it is established or not contested that the child has committed an offence.

These recommendations presuppose an ideal world. If they could be followed to the letter and reciprocal action followed by social work departments, as was hoped by those who drew up the Act, the result would be a very positive step forward. Unfortunately, in the real world, things do not always work out the way they are planned.

In 1971 the Scottish Home and Health Department circulated a document to the chief constables proposing further developments in community involvement policing. This document stated: 'The Secretary of State has accepted the advice of the Police Advisory Board for Scotland that he should assist forces in intensifying the total effort which they are currently expending on various forms of police involvement in the community.' The circular goes on to indicate that there was no single form of organisation to co-ordinate such work that would suit all forces, but that the chief constables and police authorities should decide on the arrangements that suited their area best. It did, however, recommend the establishment of 'community involvement branches' whose responsibility might include some or all of the following matters:

Direct Responsibility
1. Liaison with social work departments on
   (a) matters affecting juveniles.
   (b) social welfare matters.
2. Co-operation of warning and juvenile liaison schemes.
3. Organisation of crime prevention propaganda and crime prevention panels.
4. Supervision of race relations matters generally.

Responsibility shared with Territorial Divisions
1. Fostering community involvement activities of area constables.
2. Organisation of communications with youth, tenants associations, church and other organisations.
3. Arrangement of talks to schools.
4. Arrangement of talks on police work and visits to police stations.
5. Fostering of recruitment of, and assisting in organisation of 'special constabulary'.

It was recommended by the Home and Health Department that 2 per cent of force strength should be the correct size for such departments.

It can be seen from all these instructions and reports that the Scottish police were giving very serious thought to their community role. Planning, at the highest level, had continued over a long period to decide how best to operate community policing under the new Act. We will consider how these recommendations affected Strathclyde police—the largest force in Scotland, dealing with the highest rate of crime in the country and policing some of the most deprived urban areas in Europe. The Strathclyde Force resulted from the amalgamation of six forces in 1975. The Chief Constable set up a Working Party to plan the community involvement role of the new force.

The new Community Involvement Branch was given three main responsibilities:

1. *Practical or physical crime prevention*. This involves all matters associated with the security of premises and property, organising crime prevention panels, publicity and exhibitions dealing with crime prevention, liaising with architects and planners etc.

2. *Social Crime Prevention*. This involves the processing and vetting of all reports relating to child offenders, operating the Strathclyde Police Advisory Service (see below), liaising with the Reporter, social workers and all those concerned with the problem of juvenile delinquency, and arranging talks and police projects in schools.

3. *Community Relations*. This mainly involves contact with community councils, tenants' associations, schools, councils and urban renewal projects. Race relations present no problem in Strathclyde.

The role played by the Strathclyde Police Youth Advisory Service is very similar to that of juvenile liaison. The object of the scheme is to attempt to assist potential offenders—young people under 16 years of age whose anti-social behaviour may indicate that they are likely to drift into crime—by giving them some form of voluntary supervision, encouraging them to get involved in local activities and clubs and giving the parents any assistance possible. Such young people may come to the notice of the police through their parents seeking help, or through teachers, shopkeepers or youth and community workers. In addition, patrol officers are all issued with 'contact cards'[1] on which they record their contacts with any young people that seem to be in doubtful, or unusual circumstances—such as wandering late at night, playing truant, glue-sniffing or associating with known criminals. These contact cards are a source of useful information for the Community Involvement Branch as they may be a means of initiating action to prevent the youngster getting into serious trouble. Supervision is offered to some young offenders, who have committed minor offences which are not considered to be sufficiently serious to warrant a referral to the Reporter. This supervision may be given by a community involvement officer or an area constable. In all cases, if the child does not respond to this supervision, further help will be sought. This may be referral to the Reporter, Social Work Department or psychiatric clinic. When in doubt the community involvement officers are instructed to seek such expert advice, and this procedure enables many youngsters to receive help at an early stage and perhaps prevents them from getting into more serious trouble.

Most police forces in Scotland set up similar branches and established similar procedures. Police involvement with other agencies increased greatly after the Social Work Act came into being and there is no doubt that this involvement has enabled the police to build very useful bridges between their service and the community. Unfortunately, there still exists a gap between the police who are not involved in community involvement work and sections of the community, although a system of rotating staff in Community Involvement Branches will probably gradually erode this gap. Senior officers increasingly see the value of their community involvement staff, although hostility at any rank can undermine the work being done by the Branch. One senior community involvement officer commented: 'I have far more problems with my own colleagues than I do with other agencies'. This comment was made after some harassment of youngsters by the local police in an area of high delinquency. The community involvement officers, with the co-operation of the youth workers, had managed to organise these youngsters into a committee to run a youth club—a task which they did with enthusiasm. Unfortunately, the local police were reluctant to accept that this was genuine and made a point of picking the lads up when they saw them. It was far harder convincing the local police that these youngsters were doing a good job than it was persuading the boys to behave themselves. In addition, instead of these youngsters getting a more positive attitude to the police generally, they simply discriminated between the community involvement officers and the rest—thus effectively undermining what the whole project was about.

It was tough enough for the early juvenile liaison officers, but it was, and is, much tougher for the community involvement branches. They tend to be held responsible for all the problems caused by the new Act—and it certainly has created enormous problems for the police, as well as for the rest of the community. Trying to act as a bridge between police and the social services, working out new and highly sophisticated procedures which were never clearly thought out or properly planned, is a thankless and complicated task. It is hard to try to reach a reasonable working relationship with social work departments, it is harder still to gain the necessary co-operation from fellow policemen. Any failures or mistakes on either side tend to be seen as the fault of the Community Involvement Branch and it is on them that senior officers turn their wrath—regardless of rights or wrongs. It is to be hoped that it will not be too long before all policemen accept the point made by the Chief Constable of the Central Police:

> The prevention of crime and the maintenance of law and order, assisting the public and encouraging social conscience and respect for law and order are the basic aims of the police and the means of attaining these aims must change as society itself changes. Thus community involvement is not the development of a specialist role but the fundamental task of every member of this Force.

Meanwhile, in England and Wales similar developments were taking place. In 1965 the Ingleby Committee reported and the White Paper, 'The Child, the Family and the Young Offender', was published. The Ingleby Committee made no radical recommendations and even those it did make were not regarded as acceptable by the government. In fact, the problem of the conflict between a judicial and a welfare model for juvenile offenders was never resolved, and in spite of four years' deliberation the Ingleby Committee produced nothing but suggestions for minor change, and the government was content to leave things as they were. The retention of juvenile courts was recommended but it was suggested that the age of criminal responsibility should be raised from eight to twelve years. This proposal met with serious opposition as it was considered that this would mean losing the chance of 'teaching the young offenders a lesson' by the useful penalties of fines and probation orders imposed by the courts. In fact, a compromise was reached and the age of criminal responsibility was fixed at ten years.

The White Paper proposed the idea of local family councils to deal with juvenile offenders under the age of 16 years. The police were not asked to comment on the document which was received very critically. In 1969 another White Paper was produced— 'Children in Trouble'—and this became the basis of the Children and Young Persons Act (1969). This document emphasised the importance of the family and social background's influence on children who get into trouble and highlighted the importance of preventive work with children and their families. It emphasised the fact that juvenile misbehaviour results from the process of growing up, although some has a deeper cause. Formal procedures were recommended to be reserved for situations where it was in the best interests of the child or of society. The aim of the White Paper was stated as being 'to produce a comprehensive yet flexible framework for the development of work with children in trouble over the coming years'.

The main proposals of the White Paper were:

1. Juvenile courts should be retained.
2. Prosecution of children between ten and fourteen years old should cease and action be taken on a voluntary basis. If a child commits an offence and his parents are not providing adequate care, protection and guidance, or the offence indicates that he is beyond parental control, it should be possible to take him to the juvenile court as in need of care, protection or control.
3. As far as possible, young people between fourteen and seventeen years old should be dealt with on a voluntary basis and recourse to the courts allowed only if one or more criteria are satisfied and the magistrate agrees. Care proceedings can be instituted until the seventeenth birthday.
4. Probation orders should cease to be legally distinct from supervision orders, children under fourteen being supervised by the local authority and from fourteen-seventeen years old by the legal authority or probation service.
5. Local authorities should provide intermediate treatment centres to replace juvenile detention centres and juvenile attendance centres.
6. Children and young persons requiring treatment away from home should be placed in the care of the local authority. The

approved school and borstal order would cease to exist.

7.   Local authorities should be responsible for developing a comprehensive system of community homes for children, in which approved schools should be included.

According to the Act, which came into effect in 1971, juveniles coming to the attention of the police can be dealt with in the following ways:

1. An order can be made requiring parent or guardian to enter into a recognisance to take proper care of the child and exercise proper control.

2. A supervision order.

3. A care order.

4. A hospital order.

5. A guardianship order.

Appeal to the courts is possible in all cases except 1.

Consultation with the police regarding this Act was minimal and no specific instructions were laid down or discussed as had been the case in Scotland. One reason for this may be that the importance and value of community policing was more apparent in a small country like Scotland where, after amalgamation, there were only eight constabularies; in a large and diverse nation such as England the importance has been less appreciated, although the situation is now changing rapidly. Most police forces in England and Wales were left to prepare their own schemes for coping with the new situation created by the Act.

We will consider the procedures adopted by the Metropolitan Police, being the largest force in England. Historically, the Metropolitan Force had shown little enthusiasm for preventive procedures—since 1931 there had been a very limited amount of cautioning—in 1966 out of 11,138 prosecutions, only 93 were cautioned. Among provincial forces the cautioning rate reached as high as 70 per cent. The Metropolitan Police investigated the Liverpool Juvenile Liaison Scheme but rejected it, party because of manpower shortage and partly because of philosophy: to quote the Commissioner, Sir Joseph Simpson 'If police take it upon themselves to deal with young offenders for a first offence or in minor cases by way of warning offenders, they may be subsequently accused. . . of having spoilt the best chance of reclamation.' In 1958 the Commissioner suggested a review of cautioning policy and in 1961 an experimental juvenile liaison project was established in the Newham area. This project was not considered successful, party because there was some confused thinking, which led to inconsistency among senior officers. In 1968 the Juvenile Bureau was established as an experiment in one division. This proved successful and, as a result, the Metropolitan Police Advisory Committee made the following recommendations:

1. That juvenile bureaus should be set up in all divisions under a Chief Inspector, responsible for all matters relating to juveniles in that division and also responsible for liaising with various local authority departments.
2. That a system for procedure with juveniles should be adopted as an alternative to charging and should embody a system of cautioning in suitable cases.

Juvenile bureau staff became responsible for gathering information about the juvenile from various relevant agencies; they paid home visits, gathering useful information to assist in the decision-making process. The duties of a juvenile bureau officer were specified as:

1. Computing a docket on each juvenile for each case allocated.
2. Checking the Force Index on juveniles and various local authority departments for background information.
3. Making home visits.
4. Compiling comprehensive reports on juveniles.
5. Submitting papers through the bureau sergeant.
6. Informing the juvenile, his parents and the officer in the case of the decision.
7. Supervising the typing of information and the application for summons.
8. Warning juveniles and parents, ensuring the officer in the case and witnesses are warned for court attendance.
9. Attendance at court to assist the magistrate.
10. Returning all case papers after the conclusion of the case.

What can the police do about the young offender?
1. He can be given an official warning.

2.   He can be prosecuted in court.
3.   Care proceedings can be instituted.
4.   No further action need be taken.

The problem of the juvenile who commits offences in association with adults caused some discussion and after a formal meeting with the Commissioner it was decided that, in the case of joint offences, juveniles could be dealt with separately by the Juvenile Bureau. Magistrates were not happy about this but agreed to a ten months experiment. After this, the scheme was reluctantly accepted. Police records are kept of all cautions until the offender is 17½ years old and then they are destroyed. The philosophy behind the Juvenile Bureau is the same as that which stimulated the changes in legislation—that a young person should have the chance of learning by experience without the harsh consequences of convictions which affect employment, travel and emigration opportunities because of childish misbehaviour.

How has the new legislation been functioning in England and Scotland? In 1972 the Institute for the Study and Treatments of Delinquency held a conference to review 'the Future of the Juvenile Courts'. At that conference the Deputy Chief Constable of Birmingham was reported to have expressed concern regarding the inadequacy of residential accommodation, the lack of trained social workers and the inadequacy of their training. He also expressed concern at the inability to take effective action against a child under 14 years, subject to a care order, who continued to commit offences, where the police received constant complaints from citizens who claimed the right of protection. Professor Cavanagh, JP, at the same conference, expressed similar anxiety, particularly about offenders whom the social services were unable to rehabilitate yet the juvenile court had no power to restrict—consequently, offences were committed with impunity and courts were as busy as before the Act. From a recent discussion programme between magistrates, police, social workers and others on BBC 2, it would appear that the situation in England and Wales has not improved since this conference.

Comments about the Scottish situation were—and are—similar. It is said that the system is failing to be fully efficient because of the shortage of trained social workers and other resources. Dr Peter Scott comments in the *British Journal of Criminology*[2] 'Is it supposed that there will ever be enough social workers? Probably not.' In a review of the Scottish scene in *Focus*,[3] J.O. Johnston, then

Director of Social Work in Glasgow, suggests that police and courts who cited the inadequacy of resources as the cause of the failure of the Act should note that this was not new and was the case under the old legislation. He goes on to question whether the failure of the old system might be due to this inadequacy of resources, and justifies changing the system by the establishment of the Panels, 'who can act as a pressure group determined to ensure that necessary resources are provided'. This article was entitled 'Five Years On'—nine years on we are still waiting! Attempts to get preventive action taken with children at risk are still met with 'Don't tell me about the ones who may get into trouble, my hands are already too full with the ones who have.'

Most people will accept that much juvenile offending is developmental and part of the process of growing up, and that concern for the welfare of the young must be the pivot of all dealings with juveniles; that the most effective way of preventing minor anti-social behaviour developing into really criminal behaviour is to catch it early and take some preventive action. Police warnings and juvenile liaison officers recognised this need many years ago. The welcome given to the Social Work (Scotland) Act and the Children and Young Persons Act (1969), was based on the impression that at last prevention was going to become a reality; that instead of young children getting caught up into the criminal justice system at a tender age, the community would take responsibility for assisting the child to develop more acceptable behaviour patterns. It was hoped that social workers, teachers, youth workers and the community at large —parents and neighbours—would all become involved in giving various forms of preventive help. One of the weaknesses has been that resources to back up the ideas of the Acts have been very thin; in addition, community action has not been stimulated to a sufficient degree —even in Scotland, where the Children's Panels have meant that far more of the community are getting involved in the problems of young offenders.

If concern to prevent a child being stigmatised by judicial action is interpreted as doing absolutely nothing about the youngster's anti-social behaviour, it is unlikely to produce anything other than more serious social problems, and that surely cannot be in the best interests of the child. We are faced at present with the tragedy that the 'cops and robbers' games that children have played throughout the ages have suddenly taken on a startling reality. Children living in crowded and deprived urban areas play 'cops and robbers' for real. If the police catch a child committing an offence, the message must be got home to that child that such behaviour is unacceptable and will lead to serious consequences. It is for parents to exert their influence on the child to ensure he does not reoffend. How one persuades some parents to do this is the 64,000 dollar question! Perhaps the old Scottish 'caution' might be considered; under Scots law, a parent of a child who had offended paid a sum of money as a 'caution' for the child's good behaviour. This money was returned to the parent if the child did not reoffend. In present day society, money seems to have more impact on some than words. One thing is certain—to allow a child to offend with impunity, to be caught by the police and to find that nothing ensues, helps neither the child nor society. Most of those involved with young people in trouble know of cases where children have built up impressive records of offending and who appear to have taken on the majesty of the law and won.

The Commissioner of the Metropolitan Police, Sir David McNee, in an address to the National Association of Boys' Clubs in July 1978, makes a similar point:

> There is a clear need to separate the criminal from welfare proceedings; and in dealing with young offenders, to make punishment the first option and treatment the second, thereby reversing the current order of emphasis and relieving some of the burden on the overstretched social work services, allowing them to concentrate their efforts on the minority who really need their help and support. The need for both punishment and treatment was implicit in the White Paper 'Children in Trouble'. That is an important point that has been lost somewhere along the way. Somewhere between alternate extremes of punitive retribution and permissive welfare lie answers which must be found. Social workers, magistrates, probation officers and police officers: all must work closer together towards solutions.

The Children and Young Persons Act (1969) and the Social Work (Scotland) Act are instruments which can and do protect many children in a constructive and positive way. This must not be forgotten —the picture is not all black. It must also be remembered that once a child gets caught up into the system of residential care, every placement makes it more likely that he will reoffend, so any action that attempts to prevent this is worthwhile. As has already been said, we do not know how to cure; at present we seem to lack the will to prevent. Progressive legislation is important, but progressive legislation that is too far ahead of resources to implement it and public opinion to back it, can accomplish little and can set up a backlash that leads to reactionary measures which prevent positive change for years to come. It is to be hoped that the two Acts, with their constructive emphasis on the welfare of the young, will not have this effect.

Notes

1. See Appendix II.
2. *British Journal of Criminology* (1975), vol. 15, no. 4.
3. *Focus* (1974), no. 33.

4 THE POLICE AND SOCIAL WORK

'Police and social work can only effectively work together insofar as they are able to respect each other and understand the problems of the other service.'[1] A correct comment but perhaps it needs to be taken further; genuine respect and understanding are difficult enough to achieve but the understanding needs to be more than of the problems each are facing. It needs to be a real appreciation of each other's role in the community. Lack of such appreciation causes each side to have stereotypes of the other. The policeman may see the social worker as a 'long-haired, anti-establishment do-gooder' who always seems to want to let off the villains the policeman has just locked up. The social worker sees the policeman as a 'tough, uncompromising and sometimes stupid reactionary' who spends his time putting people away for no good cause. It is easy to develop stereotypes if contact is rare and confined to situations where some conflict of interest is inevitable. When, in addition, policemen get involved in juvenile liaison/community relations roles, the tension increases on both sides. The social workers see the policeman as trespassing on their territory without adequate training. The policeman sees the social worker as rejecting his genuine attempts to deal with some of the many young offenders to whom social workers cannot devote the time they should, and is accordingly inclined to bitterness.

Nigel Grindrod suggests that part of the conflict arises from a semantic confusion—the term 'social work' is used incorrectly for 'social service'—and that in fact, these two functions are very different. Social service is something that all kinds of untrained people in the community are able to do and the police particularly. Social work, on the other hand, means

> the practice of a skill based on extensive training which enables one person to help others to come to terms with illness, handicap, misfortune, disadvantage etc. This help is based on an understanding of interpersonal relationships that goes beneath the

surface and the obvious to the irrational, unseen, emotional depths that motivate and drive people, often against their own will, wish or better judgement, so that by helping people to perceive what is going on within themselves they are enabled to function more effectively.

This rather idealistic definition of social work, differentiating it from social service, does give a clue to the source of some of the police-social work conflicts. At present, because of staff shortages, pressure of work and financial stringency, few social workers are able to do more than 'social service', as defined by Grindrod. To the policeman it looks very like what a lot of people do anyway with the young, including certain policemen. 'So where's the special magic of social work?' is fairly asked. The 'special magic', which more mundanely might be called 'casework', is a skill which is rarely relevant in the treatment of the average young offender. Indeed, with the present level of offending, the numbers of social workers would have to be increased to an unacceptable level to attempt any type of casework with the vast number of young offenders passing through the system. Working in the present situation, where both professional groups do social service, requires close co-operation between police and social workers, acting in complementary roles rather than conflicting roles as is too often the case at present.

Attitudes need to change on both sides: social workers have to make clear to young offenders that their anti-social behaviour is quite unacceptable to the community. Policemen must try to separate the behaviour from the individual youngster—one or two mistakes do not condemn a youngster for ever. Young offenders become confused and conflicted if they find their social worker tries to protect them from the consequences of their misdeeds and the policeman writes them off as a 'dead loss'. The skill which both agencies require is the ability to reject the anti-social behaviour but not the person. This would give hope for the youngster and he may be able to avoid further offending. When dealing with offenders the average social worker and the average policeman both aim for the same objective, namely to prevent further offending. Deeper understanding of this fact would lead to more co-operation which would, in turn, have a very positive effect on some young offenders. The conflicts that arise between professionals can only harm both the community and the individuals that all seek to serve. The social worker who mutters 'the police are fascist bastards' when one of his

clients appears to have a grievance against the police, simply aggra-
vates the problem. The policeman who allows his prejudice against
the social worker to overwhelm him into harrying some of the
clients, helps no one. Some offenders have real grievances against
the police which need to be dealt with, some social workers genuinely
try to do supervision and need help rather than harassment for their
clients. Many good, constructive, individual working relationships
exist between police and social workers but these individual relationships rarely seem to have sufficient impact to affect the system. Even
good relationships at the top of the hierarchy can have little impact
on the lower echelons where the difficulties of working together are
of far greater importance. One of the problems, of course, is that the
professionals—the police, social workers, psychiatrists etc.—pre-
sume they know what the community expects of them, what their
role is. Perhaps they are wrong and the time has come to go back to
the community and find out what service is expected from each.

The problem of non-accidental injury to children is an area where
the police and social work need to have close contact and where
differing interests are involved. Working parties who are responsible
for screening children at risk and dealing with individual cases,
involve both social workers and policemen, among other professional groups. Conflicts tend to arise and the police very often find
themselves isolated. Their responsibility is to protect the child from
further violence, and that means removing him from his violent
parents; the social workers, and probably others, tend to see the
preservation of the family unit as being of prime importance. In
some areas the police are excluded from these groups on grounds of
confidentiality. Such exclusion can only exacerbate relationship
problems, particularly when information is sought from the police
and none given in return. In areas where the exchange and co-operation is fully operative, these groups have proved a useful meeting
place; but even in such areas, conflicts may arise over action priority.
The police have to take the line 'an offence has been committed, we
must therefore take action and report the case to the Procurator
Fiscal'. The social worker complains 'if the parents are arrested the
family will have to be taken into care and this may do more harm
than the parental action'. To the policeman, who sees the child's life
as being at risk, this attitude smacks of irresponsibility; the social
worker may well have weighed up the present risk of physical injury
against the certainty of emotional damage that family breakup may
cause. Sometimes policemen are too precipitate in their action

although legally their position is indisputable. Conversely, social workers may be too laggardly. Inevitably it is the family in the middle who suffers, as is always the case in any professional disagreements that are resolved without true co-operative effort. More understanding and trust are needed so that decisions are made jointly in the best interests of the child at risk, not just in defence of a particular professional stance.

The problem of relationships between police and social work is not peculiar to Britain; it exists all over the world and it would appear that no one nation or group has really solved it. Many attempts have been, and are being, made. In America, in the state of Illinois, an interesting experiment was set up in an attempt to overcome some of the professional barriers and develop a means of diverting as many people as possible, particularly young people, outwith the criminal justice system. The experimental project was set up by Professor Harvey Treger of the University of Illinois at Chicago Circle; it was known as the Police-Social Service Project (SSP).[2] The initial aims laid down were that it should fulfil the following functions:

1. Develop a new direction in diversion at the point of contact with law enforcement; the earliest point in the criminal justice system.
2. Provide a new model for co-operative relationships between social work and law enforcement.
3. Alleviate the overloading of the criminal justice system.
4. Extend protection through the provision of a new service for non-violent and victimless offenders.

The project was set up in two experimental areas in 1970. Professional social workers and graduate social work students were placed in two middle-class community police departments. One of the ten stated objectives was 'to open channels for improved communication between law enforcement and social work'. In addition, the SSP aimed to supply an immediate, 24-hour service for non-violent offenders coming to the attention of the police. It was hoped that the project would take pressure off both courts and police. By 1974 the SSP had shown its value and eight police districts had an SSP in the local police station.

In the view of the initiators of the projects, the social workers and police officers would achieve results by working together, that neither could hope to achieve in isolation. In addition, both professional groups would contribute a new dimension to their work and find a new way of solving their clients' problems. By placing the social worker at the source of referral, i.e. the police station, it was hoped that some of the problems which undermine the treatment of offenders would be overcome. Two of the problems identified by Professor Treger were: (i) Delays in giving service—it was hoped that by being on the spot at the time of crisis, social work intervention would be more effective; and (ii) lack of authority over clients—the extra authority of the police would increase the clients' motivation and make the social worker's attitude more aggressive and less dependent on client motivation. In addition, by working together, the sharing of the information would not present the problem of confidentiality which causes so much bad feeling between police and social workers. If the police in addition are able to see the social worker in action as opposed to hearing about what he does, they may change their attitude and understand better what social work is about. Professor Treger comments 'The police are action-oriented; talk is not as convincing as action—and may even be counter-productive.'[3]

The type of problems handled by the SSP unit were runaway girls and boys, car theft, alcohol problems, family disputes; these were handled by individual casework, group therapy, family counselling. It was shown that the authority of the police did indeed act as the expected pressure, encouraging clients to co-operate, thus enabling them to appreciate the help available which they might, in other circumstances, have refused. At no time did the SSP expect to solve the underlying causes of crime; it was simply hoped that, by drawing police and social workers together, the service they gave to the community might be improved.

How effective have the Social Service Projects been? I was most impressed by the commitment to the idea of the police chiefs, some senior officers and local politicians and officials, who seemed to have developed a good basic understanding of the role of the social worker and were doing all they could to encourage the projects in their particular areas. The importance and value of strengthening the co-operation between police and social work was accepted by all of them. Many non-violent petty offenders had benefited from the intervention of the social work unit during the crisis period and had avoided the stigma of getting caught up in the criminal justice system. In addition, many social workers and social work students were developing a greater understanding of the police role—although it must be said that some were able to isolate themselves almost completely from the police environment. In one area the social worker seemed to have little or no contact with the policemen in the same building as himself and relationships were poor. On the other hand, in some areas relationships were exceptionally good. In one place the social worker was allowed to use the police vehicles to go round her district. Occasionally one felt that the process of integration had gone too far and the social worker had changed his role and become more of a policeman. Indeed, give him a gun and a uniform and he would be a cop. On the other hand, some of the police youth officers were indistinguishable from social workers. As they were not in uniform I at first presumed they were youth leaders and only after a time realised that they were in fact, policemen.

To understand and co-operate is important but to confuse roles helps no one. The policeman and the social worker have very distinct roles to play and if they get their roles confused, the client will again suffer. It has always been a criticism of juvenile liaison that the officers involved end up by forgetting that they are policeman. Sometimes they get their role so confused that they try to protect their young supervisees from the consequences of law breaking. This comment may seem unfair, but the risk is a real one. A good policeman and a good social worker fulfil distinct but connected roles. The important thing is that those involved shall understand and respect each other and thus enable each professional to function effectively in his own role for the benefit of the community. The policeman controls and he may counsel; the social worker counsels and he may control. Working as a team they can enable the community to receive the best possible service; in opposition, both will undermine the work of the other and again, the community will suffer.

There are many positive features about the Illinois police-social work projects but it is questionable whether by putting social workers into a police station, one achieves more than by making determined attempts to improve communication between departments as is done by community liaison branches. Contact does not depend necessarily on proximity, there is more to it than that. Some of the police chiefs in Illinois were very enthusiastic about the SSP and gave their full co-operation, but some seemed more inspired by the public relations aspect of the exercise than by any basic conviction. The enthusiastic backing of politicans and local officials created the same impression—genuine conviction in some cases, a good political gimmick in others. This is one of the most acute problems of all law and order issues—fashions emerge which are supported, not because the particular idea has been proved to be effective, successful or useful but because it may win votes more speedily. This attitude forces a certain degree of scepticism about many potentially positive developments in dealing with anti-social behaviour. Scepticism regarding the extent of the value of the Illinois project was reinforced by the attitude of some patrolmen. Some were cynical, some reserved judgement and many were unconverted and uncommitted to the project, maintaining that it was doing very little more than a policeman is doing anyway. 'They just go along and talk—we do that—anyone can talk—what's so special about that?' was a recurrent comment. They also felt that social workers tended to wait for the police to deal with any unpleasantness before they moved in. 'If there's a family fight they wait for us to settle it before they move in—they say that they can't do anything if there's violence going on. By the time they appear we have usually sorted out everything anyway.' In addition, the claim of the 24-hour service raised much mirth. Most patrolmen insisted that this was a myth; the social worker would not come out after hours to a call but would ask the police to arrange for the client to call the next day. They felt that they, the police, were still the only agency giving a really effective 24-hour service. While there is no doubt that some of these criticisms were based on places where the relationship between police and social worker had not developed as well as in other places, one was still left with the feeling that basic understanding and acceptance of the respective roles of police and social worker had not developed any further than in places where the two departments are in different buildings. The Illinois project certainly has had a considerable impact on the police and there are individual relationships from which good understanding and the ability to co-operate fruitfully have developed. It would not appear though, that there has been any greater impact on police-social work contact than has been effected in the United Kingdom by the 1968 and 1969 Acts in Scotland and England. The establishment of police community liaison departments has meant that certain policemen and certain social workers are being thrown together and, in some cases, are succeeding in bridging the gap that exists between the two professional groups. In Illinois the difference is that the social work profession are taking the initiative and playing a more spontaneous and active role in seeking co-operation.

Professor Treger fairly claims, at the conclusion of his first research report on the initial projects, that 'a viable relationship between the police, the social service project and community agencies has proved workable and useful', a conclusion with which few would argue. It is also important that experiments such as those in Illinois continue and develop if any real progress is to be made in developing real understanding and co-operation between police and social work.

The complaint made in Illinois, that only the police give a real 24-hour service, is one which is constantly made by the police about social workers in every country including the UK. It is a fair criticism —the organisation of the 'helping services' on a nine to five basis is totally unrealistic. People who need help, who get caught up in anti-social behaviour, domestic rows and violence involving police intervention, rarely choose office hours for their outbursts.[4] Even loneliness and fear tend to be night and holiday complaints, or complaints that become aggravated by the long hours of the night or holiday periods. These are the very times when the 'helpers' are not available. Most social work departments have an emergency service but it often fails to be really efficient and the necessary social worker is unlikely to be on call. 'They even have a notice on the door of our social work department saying call the police if this department is closed', complained one police officer—and this was not an isolated occurrence. Would a real 24-hour service, using a shift system like the police, resolve the problem? Looking at what happens in Sweden gives cause for doubt. In Stockholm there is a social work office in police headquarters and a social work radio car on 24-hour patrol. All juveniles, drug addicts, alcoholics and mentally sick persons must be handed over to social workers by the police on arrest. The 24-hour service really exists. However, it did not seem that relationships between the police and social workers were any better than anywhere else. The police in Sweden and Norway seemed very cynical about the role played by both social work and psychiatry. They have a reason for cynicism as once a person is handed over to a psychiatrist or social worker as being in need of psychiatric care, even if he has committed a crime of serious violence, the police have no role to play. This means that, should the psychiatrist decide that the offender is not in need of psychiatric treatment, regardless of the offence, he will be released. Comments made by both social workers and policemen in both Oslo and Stockholm suggest that close working relationships and mutual understanding are no more frequent than elsewhere. As a social worker commented in Stockholm: 'Where a personal relationship exists between a policeman and a social worker, co-operation will be good; where there is no personal contact, co-operation can be difficult.' This social worker went on to admit that social work seemed to exacerbate the situation, by the attitude taken in some situations. For example, in the Gothenburg area social workers can insist on having access to confidential police files but the police have no such right of access to social work files. 'Such arrangements do not encourage good relationships', she commented. In spite of the fact that in Sweden social workers and the police work in close proximity, and give the same 24-hour service, their working relationships do not seem to have progressed any further than those in the UK or the USA.

If so many different efforts to improve social work relations have such a limited impact, what else can be done to improve the situation? First, it must be said that no experiment can fail completely, some contacts are invariably made that will continue and that is sufficient justification for any experiment which aims at improving working relationships. Professional differences will always exist, not just between police and social work but between all professions involved in caring for people. Indeed, not just between professional groups, but also within groups where the acute differences that occur tend to be smoothed over by the common professional philosophy. If this sort of relationship could be encouraged between police and social workers it would be constructive. The problem of the treatment of offenders is very prone to emotive individual 'hang-ups' and all political discussion of the topic is hampered by this problem. Inevitably, in the actual practical situation such hang-ups will affect attitudes to the handling of individual cases. Unfortunately, we have little definitive research on the effectiveness of forms of treatment, and the only common factor that most people involved actively in the problem have is the combination of their professional role, and the feeling that they are not being successful in their work because they are being undermined by other professional groups. The police-social work conflict is a good example of this. Can such conflicts be reduced or eliminated?

One hopes that time will gradually encourage genuine efforts in co-operation. Training is probably the most important means of hastening the process and improving interdisciplinary contact. Fortunately, more and more people are becoming aware of this and an increasing number of interdisciplinary training courses and conferences are being organised. This aspect is dealt with in more detail in Chapter 7. In addition, there are many experimental projects which involve police and social workers, all of which contribute in some degree to the process of increasing understanding by increasing contact. The more contact can be encouraged by working together in many different situations, as opposed to contact in situations where conflict of role is particularly obvious, the more chance there is of increasing understanding. The latest experiment being tried by the Devon and Cornwall Constabulary is the use of exchange placements between the Force and the social services departments. Police constables do periodic placements in the social services department and social workers do corresponding placements in police stations. It is a very new scheme and is taking place in an area which is comparatively free from the sort of pressures caused by heavily populated and deprived urban populations. But if some of the conflicts of view that arise, even in relatively tranquil areas, can be shown to be alleviated by this sort of co-operative effort, then surely it points a way that should be followed in other areas?

There is an urgent and desperate need to build bridges that are effective on a wide scale between the various professional groups that are involved with offenders, and nowhere more than between social work and the police. With an escalating crime rate, an undermanned police force, a shortage of social workers and a community that is unable or unwilling to really get involved in effective action, professional groups must co-operate and give effective leadership. No one profession will ever solve the problems of law and order, but lack of co-operative effort will certainly aggravate these problems to the detriment of the life of all in the community.

Notes

1. Nigel Grindrod, *Focus* (February 1974).
2. H. Treger, 'Crime and Delinquency' in H. Treger, D. Thomson and G.S. Jaech *A Police-Social Work Team Model* (July 1974), pp. 281-9.
3. 'Social Work in Police Departments', *Social Work* (September 1973).
4. Since the time of writing, Strathcyde Social Work Department has introduced a social work standby service, operating from 5 p.m. to 9 a.m. Access to this service by members of the public is by Freephone. It is intended for emergencies and acute distress situations only.

5 COMMUNITY INVOLVEMENT

Police involvement in community projects has been a special feature of policing in parts of Scotland, particularly the west and central belt, for the past twenty years. The west of Scotland suffers from a very high level of social deprivation and poor housing; in Glasgow, for example, it has been estimated that there are 13,000 acres of multiple deprivation. An inevitable correlate of such deprivation is a high level of crime, in some areas as high as 20 per cent above the national average, and many other social problems. A study of Glasgow by the Corporation Planning Department in 1972, 'Areas of Need', identified the city as having a higher level of overcrowding, small sub-standard housing, morbidity, infant mortality and other social ills than most urban conurbations in Britain. An EEC commission, reporting in 1977, considered that the west of Scotland had the worst housing conditions in Europe.

Typical symptoms of such areas of multiple deprivation are inadequate amenities, neglected gardens and open spaces, vandalism, unemployment, sickness and poverty, truancy, and poor quality of public services such as refuse, transport, schooling, policing and housing maintenance. Residents live in a state of strain and apathy; many are afraid to leave their homes empty because of housebreaking (frequently by neighbours). Many people keep dogs which are usually large and uncontrolled and rove round the area in packs, terrorising local residents and visitors. Such areas may house as many as 50,000 people and some lack even a local shop; what shops there are, are frequently bricked up, covered with spray paint and present an appearance of neglect. Most telephone kiosks have been removed. Those that remain are heavily vandalised and rarely in working order. Such conditions have existed for many years in urban areas; it is only recently that attempts have started to remedy the situation.

In many parts of England and the USA such areas of deprivation are often inhabited largely by coloured immigrants but, apart from skin colour, there is little difference in the problems which the residents both face and present. There is a tendency for every such area to be regarded as 'the worst one' by local people, who find it hard to believe such areas exist elsewhere. The police patrolling a particularly deprived, all black area in Chicago, found it hard to accept that similar areas existed in Scotland, the only difference being skin colour and the absence of guns. They felt that the large dreary blocks of flats, dirty passages and vandalised elevators, rubbish and graffiti were typical of their black ghettos, forgetting that there are many such white ghettos in the world.

Police attitudes and feelings about such areas seem the same everywhere; impatience, disgust ('they live like animals'), anger both with the people who live in such areas and those who allow such conditions to exist; despair for the future—'what hope have their children, growing up in these conditions with adults who don't care?'; but, underlying the anger, compassion for the young who never have a chance.

The police have a particular problem in areas of deprivation, whether the colour of skin is black or white. It is here that they have to deal with many people who are at variance with the generally accepted norms and means of social control. This variance may be inherent in the local sub-culture, as in deprived urban areas in Scotland, or may result from differing immigrant cultures taking over, as in many parts of England. It is inevitable in these areas that resentment against the establishment, the lawmakers, is focused on the police as the visible embodiment of the law, leading to a high level of anti-police feeling. When there are additional problems, such as poor communication because of language difficulties, tensions soon build up and incidents explode. Such incidents tend to attract a disproportionate amount of attention when they occur in black areas.

In 1957 the Chief Constable of Greenock, David Gray, established a juvenile liaison scheme in his area. He became increasingly concerned at the hopelessness of his officers' efforts as they struggled to have some impact on the anti-social habits of the young in the area. He realised that these youngsters were living in conditions of great deprivation and that unless something was done about these conditions, his officers were wasting their time. He approached Greenock Corporation with proposals for a pilot project to be undertaken in a particularly depressed area which had a high crime rate and a high criminal population. This area was known as the Weir Street-Ladyburn area. Mr Gray pointed out to the

Corporation that many youngsters were getting involved in petty crime and vandalism in the area 'not because of innate badness but because those around them had little respect for property or law and order'. He suggested that this area be selected and that 'concentrated attention be given to it by local authority services, the churches, teachers, police and others to produce a better environment for the children to play and grow in'. Mr Gray suggested environmental improvements should be undertaken in the area, and offered to put in local constables to police the area and win the confidence of the people, particularly the children. He emphasised that making improvements to the environment was only part of the battle, these improvements had to be maintained and it would be some time before the area would stabilise.

The project was put into action. The houses were renovated and restored; the area was landscaped, trees and play areas were developed. Refuse collection was improved and house maintenance was speeded up, any damage being rectified as quickly as possible. A resident's association was set up and clubs and other facilities organised. The improvements took time, trees were sometimes damaged and had to be replaced, not once but several times. The local police officers became familiar in the area and developed useful and constructive relationships with the local people. Gradually, the area improved and the level of crime fell. Twenty years later this area shows positive change. The houses are still in good condition, the play areas are relatively free of damage and the pleasant clusters of trees give the area some character. It is no longer notorious for its high crime rate.

Mr Gray explained the project as being 'common sense'. He could not hope to overcome the problem of crime in the area without some change in the environment and without the full co-operation of other local agencies. The police acted as initiators in this project, being in the forefront of the problems it was throwing up, accepting that high crime and high deprivation go together and that to deal with the former one must tackle the latter at the same time. It was also hoped that by putting community involvement officers into areas of new public sector housing, the police would contribute towards the prevention of crime in such areas. This hope has been fulfilled in some cases, and areas such as Ravenscraig in Greenock and Linwood in Paisley remain relatively free from some of the problems which beset such areas.

This project was one of the first and earliest forms of social crime prevention put into action by the police. Then, as now, many police officers considered that this was not a role for the police to play. They missed the important point which Mr Gray identified, that crime does not occur in isolation nor can it be dealt with effectively as a separate entity. Environmental factors aggravate the problems facing both police and local people. The rather simplistic, and optimistic, approach of the old-fashioned policeman that all that was needed was to catch the villains was unlikely to be particularly effective in such an environment. In order to deal effectively with the symptom of anti-social behaviour, the police in Greenock accepted that the underlying problems, bad housing and social neglect, had to be tackled. Hostility within the police towards these ideas has presented such projects with almost as many problems as hostility from other agencies. A young policeman involved in a community project summarised the problem:

> How can we hope to get anywhere with these people, particularly the kids, if the 'heavy mob' move in behind us and lean on them for petty things. It simply means they continue to regard the police with distrust and just view us as the exceptions—the 'goodies'. If we cannot win their respect and trust for the police as a whole we might just as well pack up and go home.

A fair point about the manner in which action is sometimes taken, although it must be remembered that the 'heavy mob' have as important a role in preventive policing as the community involvement officers. When two branches of the service conflict in this way, it seems time that both begin to ask themselves what they are trying to achieve.

A Strathclyde Police Working Party report on the possible role of the police in environmental improvement projects makes the comment: 'The most perturbing aspect we found in this policing was the animosity being engendered towards the project by some officers employed in more conventional forms of policing and we are in no doubt that the attitude of those involved is a reflection of attitudes adopted by senior officers who should know better.' The report goes on to say

> Great care must be taken to recruit the correct type of personnel who, if at all possible, have local knowledge of the area and the community. Ample evidence is available of men who were not only non-volunteers, but in some cases detailed such duties (a)

against their wishes (b) without prior consultation and (c) as a convenient means of removing them from other 'situations' within their areas. Taking into account the additional community involvement role which will be expected of a project team in regenerating their community the selection of team supervisors is of paramount importance. Research has shown that the leadership and community involvement posture adopted by senior officers is contagious and generally reflected in the attitude of subordinates. The support of divisional commanders and senior officers must be wholeheartedly demonstrated to all ranks. This vital aspect will often determine the success or failure of a project.

This police working party report put its finger on the most important aspect of any community policing experiment; without this wholehearted support from the top, any efforts at street level will lack conviction. Community involvement policing cannot be used as simply a public relations exercise in any project. Such an approach will do more harm than good.

Decisions by the police to initiate such projects are usually made on the basis of high crime rates. For example, in a town of 95,000 people, one area was shown to throw up 50 per cent of all offenders in the town. This area contained only 9,000 inhabitants. In some cases the residents of such areas initiate projects by seeking police help with their problems. The help sought is usually extra police resources, but most police chiefs accept that placing extra police resources into such an area is, as an isolated activity, not particularly constructive. Three stages are needed. Firstly, planning with other local agencies, looking at environmental needs, facilities for young people and ways of stimulating local community action. Once the plans have been agreed, the second stage of putting environmental improvements into effect is initiated and, at the same time, police and other agencies set about stimulating the local population into taking positive action. The final stage is the development, from this co-operation, of local clubs, community centres, football pitches, play groups and other such community activities. In addition, local services are improved. For example, in one such project area, there was no bus service as the area was considered so bad the bus drivers would not go into it. There was also only a spasmodic refuse service and even the police presence amounted to a speedy panda patrol. Here a local police office was established as a first step and gradually local services were improved. One interesting experiment was the siting of a telephone kiosk in the new police office. For the first time local people had access to a telephone that remained in working order. In the early days of this experiment, there were constant queues waiting to use the telephone—a novel way of bringing the local people into contact with the police. Unfortunately, the financial restrictions caused cutbacks in the area and this resulted in an upsurge of anti-social behaviour in the community. This illustrates the difficulty of effective remedial action in areas of multiple deprivation where 'impossible communities' have been created by deliberate housing policy. The 'dumping' of problem families into communities which are already overburdened with overwhelming problems has created many of these 'impossible communities'. Now the political climate demands action, and a great deal of time and many millions of pounds are being poured into rectifying some of these mistaken policies and regenerating some of these areas, sometimes an impossible task. An additional problem is that political support demands an immediacy of return. If this fails, so does the political will. Unfortunately, regenerating most areas of multiple deprivation is a very long-term process and one that cannot be hurried or handled economically. It is questionable whether many politicians will be prepared to give the support necessary for such expensive long-term planning.

Two separate networks are necessary for successful projects.[1] One such network involves the Scottish Development Department, senior regional and district officials, environmental improvement department, consultant architects, contractors' representatives, senior police and fire officers. The other network involves regional and district authorities, local councillors, the department of social security, departments of health, lighting, cleansing, social work, community development, education, leisure and recreation, gas, electricity, water, the GPO, site agents, transport, fire and ambulance, churches, youth clubs, community associations, local shopkeepers and police. Every stage requires careful planning; for example, contractors involved in environmental improvements must plan their activities with great care, ensuring that equipment is stored in vandal-proof corrals. Rubble must not be left around to tempt local youngsters into some target practice which may undo completed work. The fact that repeated restoration may sometimes be needed is often the most difficult point to get over to those involved. It takes time to overcome the tendency to destroy, and trees may be damaged, windows broken and grass destroyed at first. If damage is left unattended, it will incite further damage and the project will fail. Good and speedy maintenance is vital for every developmental project. The police are most likely to be aware of damage and be able to pressurise the relevant authority to deal with it quickly.

The most important aspect of any community project is the involvement of the local people. If this involvement is not stimulated the project will fail. Residents' associations are usually established, sometimes stimulated by the police who actively participate in the association, sometimes by the local residents who take the initiative. A good measure of the success of a project is the level of community responsibility taken by the local people. This is sometimes particularly difficult to stimulate when the project has been imposed on the area. Some local people will come forward but it is often the same ones who keep volunteering.

One of the most successful projects developed from local action in a particularly deprived area in Greenock. A group of young people were fed up with having nowhere to meet and being constantly harassed by the police for congregating on street corners. They approached the community involvement officer and asked his help in getting a hut which they could use as a club room. A hut was supplied and the young people erected it and took full responsibility for running it, with the support of the local people, social workers and community workers. Crime, vandalism and disorder were dramatically reduced in the area and many constructive activities developed. A group was set up to play at discos and became a focus for the young. These youngsters are now very ready to discuss their past and some of the anti-social behaviour in which they have been involved. They were all ready to admit they had been in borstal, prison and other institutions, that they had been involved in thieving and violence. The fact that sometimes their misdeeds were written up in the papers caused them no concern at all, even although the offence might involve serious violence.

If we were never going to do anything much in our lives or be noticed, it seemed good to get your name in the paper as a hard man, to have people read about the tough things you have done. Now its different—now we are able to achieve something. The youngsters growing up here have something to look forward to, they can get involved in sport, join the club or the band, they don't need to do bad things to get noticed.

The lad who said this was now doing a social work training. He probably oversimplified the situation but there was truth in his statement. Crime and vandalism were dramatically reduced in the area. His statement illustrates the hopelessness of trying to deal with criminal activities in areas of high deprivation. Trying to reduce crime and neglecting the realities of the daily lives of the residents of such areas, will achieve little. Expecting conformity from people who have nothing to lose, whose sub-culture is naturally anti-social in establishment terms, and who are consequently anti-police, is expecting the impossible. The changes that have been achieved in this particular area have been slow and fraught with problems, but slowly a more realistic community spirit is developing. One of the results of all these changes is a considerable improvement in the relationship between the police and the local community.

In Strathclyde and other parts of Scotland, police projects have tended to concentrate on whole housing areas that are regarded as being either seriously deprived or both deprived and having a high crime rate. Most of those involved in such projects point out that, although a whole area may be identified as being deprived and criminal, when the actual criminal records are analysed, it is usually noticed that those involved in criminal activity amount to a small group within the area, maybe involving one or two streets and the same group of families whose names keep reappearing in police files. For example, in the deprived area of Scotland already referred to, which was producing 50 per cent of crime in the town, it was in fact 60 families out of the 9,000 residents who were responsible for most of the anti-social behaviour. Similar patterns have been demonstrated in other such areas which suffer from the label of being 'criminal areas'. This reputation is earned by a minority of residents but it is a reputation which causes tremendous problems for everyone living in the area. It is not easy to get a job if your address is in a 'criminal area' and the problems of daily living are multiplied by such a handicap.

The Devon and Cornwall Constabulary noted and have used exactly this sort of phenomenon in some of their preventive policing experiments. There was concern at the escalation of criminal incidents over an eight year period, particularly as a large amount of these incidents involved youngsters under 17 years of age. It was decided that some form of programme must be instituted to prevent young people getting involved so heavily in crime. The Crime Prevention Support Unit (CPSU) was set up and the first task undertaken was to produce a spot map of addresses of known offenders and offences, in order to identify areas from which offenders were coming. It was hoped to find out if different areas produced different patterns of offending. In fact this exercise demonstrated that the reputation for delinquency which was held by some of these estates was unjustified; that streets with a high crime rate were alongside streets where there was little anti-social activity. The blanket reputation given to an estate was unjustified and was earned for it by the behaviour of a small group living within a particular street or locality.

Once the CPSU had identified an area as being highly criminal, they presented the statistics to the local government officer responsible for providing and co-ordinating youth activities within the city. He was able to see that the juveniles most at risk resided in areas that had the fewest youth activities. As a result he was able to take some action in redeploying resources, and other agencies also came forward to contribute. However, when making decisions about the needs of a particular area the police considered that their most important source of information was the local people and they sought to find out how the local community felt about their neighbourhood and the problems it presented. Approaches were made to residents in the high crime areas, they were given the information the police held regarding the crime in their area and asked for help in combating the problem. Through neighbourhood and parent-teacher meetings, the local interest was activated and the police were able to recruit volunteers to assist them in implementing recreational programmes for the young during the summer holidays. In one such experiment the police developed a recreational project close to two high risk areas, and gradually the local people came forward and took over the scheme, under the leadership of a police officer.

Another experiment set up by the CPSU was the establishment of an action group, consisting of representatives from various local agencies who, with the police, worked together in providing local amenities. As a result of their activities, two youth clubs were established and the professionals working together achieved a greater understanding of each other's role and attitudes. This improved working relationship could only be beneficial for the area.

As a result of these experimental schemes the Devon and Cornwall Constabulary Crime Prevention Support Unit created a community policing consultative group, which consisted of representatives from transport, press, education, highways, health, social security, employment, licensed victuallers, politicians, engineers, churches, trade unions, magistrates and technical services. This group has the following terms of reference:

1. To provide a community forum for considering ways in which to reduce crime by social as well as police action, and for sharing our respective problems and initiatives.
2. To identify community needs and formulate possible action through a multi-disciplinary approach and report when necessary to other bodies.
3. To maximise the use of available resources.
4. To review, support and monitor local community initiatives.
5. To determine and promote training for a programme with a multi-disciplinary approach.

This group has, to use the words of Superintendent Moore who is the initiator of the project, 'opened up lines of communication and a new field of crime prevention'.

These experiments in community policing by the Strathclyde police and the Devon and Cornwall Constabulary all take place in areas where the problems are crime and deprivation, but in no part of either police area are there any immigrant areas of any significance. The problem of race is practically non-existent in both Scotland and the west country. Because of this, police forces which have large areas of racial minority settlement would probably maintain that their problems are different.

In London, the Metropolitan Police can claim to have the greatest problem, in terms of racial ghetto areas, in Britain. The Metropolitan Police community liaison officers have the responsibility of working in areas of high immigration, most of which are also areas of high deprivation and crime. The CLO participates in community associations, attempting to promote good relationships between the police and the community. The suspicion regarding the police felt by the immigrant population is much the same as the suspicion felt by any deprived urban community. The element that contributes to the heightening of tension is the colour of the skin, but it must be realised that a young policeman in a deprived area of Scotland, and many other 'white' areas of Britain, is as much at risk from the local population when he seeks to make an arrest as a policeman in a black area of London or Birmingham. For example, in a deprived area of Strathclyde a near riot developed after the police had arrested a local criminal. Two hundred local people attacked the police station which contained five policemen. Not a subject for headline news because all those involved had white skins. Such an incident occurring in a black area would certainly merit headlines and would be regarded as a 'racial' incident. It would have implications for other immigrant areas and would increase anti-police attitudes far outside the area concerned. By exaggerating the racial element in such incidents, both sides involved become more tense and suspicious and the risk of escalation increases. When a crowd of black youngsters gets out of hand it is very easy for the police to over react. It is equally easy for any police reaction to such a situation to be identified as anti-black. The same type of incident involving white youths may be handled in the same way and may aggravate anti-police feeling, but it is unlikely that the political overtones, highlighted by the media, will be of importance. The police have to respond when group disorders occur and measuring the level of response must be a commander's nightmare. Too small a squad will put his officers at risk, too big a squad may result in protests which will damage police-public relations. It is only by knowing the local area, by having constructive contacts with the local community, by taking advice from, for example, the local policemen or CLO, that this problem of how to respond can be handled without risk of causing further problems. Community liaison officers, community involvement officers, and home beat officers all comment that there are times when they should be consulted before such incidents are dealt with, and they could then ensure that some of the damaging consequences of mishandling could be avoided. Such incidents demonstrate the danger of separating the 'community policeman' from the rest of the force. Any confrontation between the police and groups of youngsters, students, coloured communities, deprived communities can, if mishandled, blow up out of all proportion and undo years of patient building-up of good relations. The fact that no blame can be attached for over reaction does not mean that it should be dismissed as 'one of those things'. Quite apart from any other factor, it makes the enthusiasm of the CLO, CIO or home beat officer wear thin.

We have been looking at some of the ways in which police forces try to assist in developing community co-operaion in deprived urban areas. This work is remedial and is dealing with the symptoms of the urban disease. Let us see if there are ways in which this disease can be prevented and what role the police can play in such prevention. The basic disease in urban areas of Britain, America and other parts of

Europe springs from similar roots. Inner cities deteriorate and are redeveloped. This results in a destructive process for local communities, some of whom will be left behind in the twilight areas and some of whom will be decanted to new areas. Decanted is an impersonal word which describes well the impersonal process involved in fulfilling planning for cities, rather than planning for communities and people. Old areas become run down and the twilight population move in—squatters, vagrants, absconders. In many parts of urban America the sign of a deteriorating area is the change in the racial composition of the population, because too often the deprived have black skins. In Britain the problems presented are very similar, even if the skin colour is different. Once urban areas deteriorate, crime becomes rampant, the area becomes a hideout for criminals, an area to be avoided by the law-abiding. I was told that there are parts of Chicago where even the telephone company and the Salvation Army will not enter by day or night. Such a situation could develop in British cities. The power failure in New York in 1977 demonstrated the seething anti-social attitudes underlying the thin veneer of socialisation. This is the state of the old areas that are being emptied. What happens in newly developed areas? Generalisation is dangerous; some new estates are havens for previously deprived people. Better housing and amenities develop community feeling and anti-social behaviour decreases. Sadly, new estates are too often badly planned, lacking adequate amenities, cut off from city centres; children find they have lost their friends, women lack companionship and support and become marooned in their new homes; men have long distances to travel to work, and family life suffers. Breaking up communities to create new housing estates damages the social fabric of cities if it is not done with care and forethought. Frequently, the sheer physical layout of a new housing estate encourages the sort of anti-social behaviour that new housing is supposed to combat. For example, the Hulme area in Manchester where, because of the design and planning, this recent project, only in existence for ten years, is a source of constant problems. Crime is rampant —there is a 40 per cent greater chance of being murdered if you live in this area than in any other part of the city. The only solution the local authority can produce is to knock it down. This is not an isolated case. Such problem areas, doomed to be demolished before the houses are even paid for, exist in many urban areas. London, along with other cities, has the problem of high rise flats and shopping areas that are so badly designed that they encourage shoplifting, mugging and housebreaking. In such areas, the local police find that shoplifting by young children has reached almost epidemic proportions. The shops lay out their goods to encourage impulse buying and, unfortunately, this also encourages impulse thieving. The kids run off and get into the long corridors of the flats and quickly disappear. Bag snatching and personal violence happens in such areas, because the very design of the building makes adequate surveillance by the police or the local community impossible — everywhere is huge and impersonal.

Oscar Newman,[2] in *Defensible Space*, demonstrates the impact which architecture and planning have on social problems. He maintains that some building layout and the materials used actually encourage crime and vandalism. Large, impersonal estates make surrounding areas so public that residents fail to develop any sense of community or personal responsibility. In addition, strangers can gain access to such areas without being noticed, and this encourages criminals and vandals. Long, impersonal walkways and corridors with inadequate lighting that are not overlooked by any dwellings are natural encouragements to committing crime.

In a study of vandalism in urban housing areas by Sheena Wilson,[3] the importance of the physical environment's impact on the local community is highlighted. When there are, in addition, large concentrations of children and problem families, crime and vandalism is likely to be rife. Informal social control is impossible in large impersonal areas which have a high child density. The police cannot hope to be everywhere, and the chances of their being on the spot to prevent vandalism and petty crime are remote. Overcrowded urban estates need more than efficient policing. 'More policemen on the beat' may be politically sound, but it is doubtful that it can be really effective in combating the sort of problems thrown up by bad design and poor planning.

Careful planning and the involvement of the police with architects, planners, sociologists, housing managers and policy planners can lead to the development of areas where both the environment and the social mix will develop a healthier social climate. It is a new role for the police and one that has considerable implications for the future. Catching and treating criminals is only one aspect of crime prevention, and one that has not proved particularly effective. Perhaps planning environments, cutting down opportunities for crime, planning communities rather than housing estates, may be a means of developing informal social controls within communities and giving the police the support which is vital if their task is to be possible.

The Strathclyde Police Regional Working Unit on Community Involvement which was set up to plan for the Community Involvement Branch in the newly amalgamated force makes the following comment:

> There has been, in our view, a reluctance on the part of the police in the past to involve themselves or concern themselves with the causes of crime and we see as much justification for considering, for example, in the preventive sense, the inadequate provision of play areas or leisure activities for young people in housing areas as in advising building architects on 'in built' security measures. The modern approach to crime prevention should embrace all these factors.

Community involvement by the police does not always follow the pattern described above. In 1975 the Cheshire Constabulary became concerned about what happened to the young people they had cautioned, particularly because they noted that 50 per cent of all crime committed in their force area was the work of youngsters under 17 years of age. Juvenile liaison was not regarded as appropriate and, in addition, it was considered that the force had insufficient manpower for such a scheme. It was therefore decided to seek the help of the public, who, in the view of the Cheshire police, must take responsibility for dealing with crime. No single service can hope to achieve any real success without this support but it was felt that if the other services, education, probation, and the social services, cooperated with the police, something might be achieved. A local committee was formed, chaired by a police officer, including among its members a social services director, a probation officer, a representative from education, a member of the juvenile court, clergy and local people. The police take responsibility for the day-to-day running of the project and the committee meets quarterly. Volunteers were sought from the public to give some attention to first-time offenders who have received a caution from the police. Originally the scheme was restricted to first-time offenders only but as it has progressed, second and third-time offenders have been placed with members of the public.

Supervision may take the form of a supportive friendship, developing a particular interest or involvement in a sport. For example, a married couple who are tug-of-war enthusiasts have run several teams consisting entirely of young delinquents. Another couple who are swimming instructors have several youngsters placed with them who are involved in competitive swimming. Some volunteers are ordinary housewives, some have special skills which are of interest to particular youngsters. Some volunteers may take a lad to a football match on a Saturday, others may simply give a youngster the sort of friendly attention he is not getting at home. There are no special guidelines or rules, procedure is left to the discretion of the volunteer. There are regular meetings held every month for the volunteers when problems and ideas are exchanged.

The police officers involved in the scheme feel that it has proved very successful. They have only had about four failures in the cases placed for supervision, and the enthusiasm of the volunteers, even when they have had to wait for a long time to have a youngster assigned to them, has continued and grown. Occasionally a volunteer has found that he cannot get on with the youngster assigned to him, sometimes a parent has objected. No placements are made without parental approval, and the police always introduce the youngster to the volunteer in the youngster's home.

This interesting project, which has become known as the 'aunts and uncles' scheme, seems a constructive way of involving the community in the problems confronting the police with young offenders, and stimulating the sort of community support and responsibility which might be expected to divert some youngsters from further offending. As the Cheshire police realised, the offending cannot be taken in isolation. The child is responding to the pressures and strains of his environment, and to deal with the offence and neglect the needs of the child may often be a wasted effort. To prevent further offending more is needed than simple police intervention and a caution, and to throw the effort back onto the community would seem exactly the role that the police should take. The continuing support and involvement in the project of the Juvenile Bureau enables the police to establish and maintain a constructive link with both the other services involved and with the community.

Another example of community involvement by the police comes from Sweden. The project resembles the Scottish model, although there is no necessity for the sort of environmental improvements that are such a vital part of community projects in Scotland. The Stockholm police became concerned about the high crime rate in an area to the north of Stockholm. It was an area containing many immigrants,

Turks, Finns and Italians, and was regarded as a deprived community. The housing consists of blocks of flats. There are relatively well kept play areas and little evidence of vandalism, sub-standard housing or environmental neglect. The children appeared clean and well cared for and it was difficult to accept this area as being deprived. Nevertheless, in Swedish terms, it presented social problems which warranted special attention.

A police office was established in a basement flat in one of the blocks. Three police officers were attached there with the responsibility for establishing good relationships with the local people, particularly the young. These officers visit schools and youth clubs, run activities in both clubs and in the police office, and make contact with the social services and the teachers. Two teachers came into the police office to translate for me and it was clear that very good relationships exist between them and these local officers. All Swedish policemen carry guns but these officers are not armed. They try to avoid getting involved in making arrests and if trouble occurs they call in the mobile support squad. They consider that if they got involved in arresting local people, their chances of making constructive relationships with the local community would be undermined. This attitude suggests that these officers are insecure in their police role and see it as conflicting with their present role. Taking effective action as a police officer when the occasion demands it should not destroy relationships with the community. Inability to handle such a situation may undermine what they are trying to do. The three officers had been carefully selected for this job and were obviously very enthusiastic about their role. They saw themselves as establishing a positive image for the police in a community that tended to be very anti-establishment. This effort seemed very dependent on the individual officer, and they were left to themselves to plan their time and their activities.

In Norway another type of community action, indirectly supported by the police, exists in Manglerud on the outskirts of Oslo. It is known as the Olso Motor Centre. It consists of a large building, erected by young people on the edge of the fiord. This building, which is jointly financed by the police, the community and the motoring organisations, contains a youth club, facilities for repairing cars and motor bikes, training areas for cars and facilities for boats. The project is run by community workers. Youngsters are referred there for any offences involving cars or motorbikes. The building has a non-alcoholic bar. The problem of teenage drinking is serious in Oslo and great stress is laid on helping the youngsters at the Centre to develop sensible drinking habits. The police have a very close relationship with the community workers at the Centre and if incidents occur with groups of youngsters congregating on motor-bikes and causing trouble, the police call up the Centre and the community workers go out on their bikes and attempt to interest the youngsters in attending the Centre. It is felt that if they can persuade some of these anti-social groups to attend the Centre, to take an interest in maintaining and repairing their bikes and generally getting involved in the activities of the Centre, they may be prevented from getting caught up in further trouble.

This project has the advantage of a large open space in which to focus its activities, with plenty of space for cars and bikes and the fiord for boating. The wide range of practical skills encouraged at the centre make it of particular value for young offenders who so often lack any skill at all. Although the police involvement tends to be rather indirect, the local officers have established good relationships with the community workers which brings them closer together and gives the police a useful link with the community.

Can all these projects be regarded as forms of crime prevention, a useful investment of police resources? If a reduction in the level of criminal activity is a measure of success, some projects can claim to have succeeded. Most have not yet been in existence long enough for such judgements to be made with any degree of conviction. Initial dramatic drops in crime levels are unlikely to be maintained. In addition, while crime may be reduced in project areas, similar reductions do not occur in neighbouring areas. With the increase in amenities and environmental improvements, it is reasonable to expect a sustained reduction in the number of nuisance offences such as vandalism, breach of the peace, etc. With the increase in community feeling and integration, housebreaking is likely to be reduced although this may simply be a local phenomenon at first.

Such changes, though, cannot be expected in the short term. Breaking bad habits is a slow and expensive procedure but worth the effort in the long run, as was demonstrated by the continuing success of the very first project in Greenock. It is easy for the changes to remain purely cosmetic and superficial. To really change anti-social habits, to have a real impact on the local sub-culture, is a much slower process. Unfortunately, there is a tendency to dismiss any ideas that do not have an immediate effect as worthless. Most local authorities expect quick returns on their investments and are not prepared to accept that changing local sub-cultures is a generation process. Children who have grown up accustomed to thieving and other anti-social behaviour, whose families accept and even connive at such behaviour, are unlikely to be changed overnight. Involving such youngsters in a variety of activities, giving them constructive outlets for their energies, will start a process. It would seem that a lot more attention should be given to the young mothers and toddlers if any lasting change is to be affected. Without such an attempt to influence the younger ones, efforts with the present youth are unlikely to achieve any lasting impact. It is through the young mothers and the rising generation that real change will be effected.

If crime can be reduced, it is good for morale—but that is a very narrow and limited objective. Improving the quality of life in deprived urban areas is inevitably a slow and often heartbreaking process, that depends for its success on the active co-operation of all local services, of which the police are but one. By their contribution to such projects the police become involved in the total life of the community and will thereby see and understand the local background and problems more fully, and also be seen and understood by both the local community and other agencies. The prevention of crime involves tackling some of the underlying ills of society which cause escalating crime rates. It seems implicit in the police role that they have a part to play in this. Because the police service in Britain is under strength it would seem even more important that they should seek to stimulate all the community support possible. The more overstretched the police resources are, the more they need the community to help them. Officers involved in community projects can make the traditional police role more effective—if there is real understanding and co-operation within the police force itself.

Notes

1. Strathclyde Police Working Party Report, 1976.
2. Oscar Newman, *Defensible Space* (Architectural Press, 1973).
3. Sheena Wilson, 'Vandalism and "defensible space" on a London housing estate' in R.V.G. Clarke (ed.), *Tackling Vandalism* (1978), HORV Study no. 47.

6   THE POLICE AND THE SCHOOLS

One of the ways in which the police made contact with the young in the days before 'lollipop' men and panda cars, was by the attention given to school crossings and road safety. The policeman escorted children across the road, he got to know many of them—and their parents—he chatted to them informally and often became a friend and adviser. Many a parent would waylay the policeman on traffic duty near the school for a chat if they were worried about some form of misbehaviour by their children and, in this way, police and community got to know each other better. The coming of the 'lollipops' put a stop to this contact and, by so doing, probably put a stop to one of the most useful informal contacts and learning situations regarding the police role to which children were exposed. It is symptomatic of the small ways in which police contact with the community has gradually been eroded by manpower shortages, specialisation and mechanisation. Because such informal contacts no longer exist, special efforts have to be made to restore contact with the young and impressionable.

For many years the police have visited schools giving talks, lectures and film shows on the subject of road safety. This has always been a 'safe', non-controversial role which has been readily accepted by most senior officers; the schools have always accepted it as important. The only problem that has arisen in this area has been with local authorities on whom rests the statutory responsibility for road safety, and who therefore sometimes see the police as trespassing on their territory.

The rising crime rate amongst the young, the increase of group disorder, combined with the shortage of police manpower and the resulting increasing alienation of the police from the community, particularly the younger age group, caused many senior officers to think about ways of remedying the situation. They realised that the children are the citizens and parents of the future, they are the most important group in the community, and if the police were to lose touch with this group, the future would be bleak.

The Sussex police have been pioneers in police-school liaison; in 1966 the first police school liaison officers were appointed, initially part-time, having operational responsibilities as well. In a letter to the Police Committee, the Chief Constable commented:

> There is a good deal of merit in forming closer links between the police and the schools which should lead to an increased understanding of each other's problems and aims, which is scarcely possible when the police only visit the schools when someone is in trouble.

This is an important point as tensions have always tended to arise between police and schools regarding the handling of offences committed on school property; many teachers prefer to handle episodes of anti-social behaviour by invoking school discipline rather than by calling on the police. Part of the problem lies in that the teachers, although increasingly concerned at the escalation of crime and violence amongst their pupils, are uncertain how to handle this without making the situation worse. If they call on the police too often, they may undermine their own authority and simply aggravate the situation. The important thing is that teachers and police co-operate; if they are in conflict regarding the handling of particular situations or individuals, the children will quickly pick this up and it may encourage anti-authority attitudes which will result in problems for all.

In 1969 the Sussex police reappraised their pilot scheme and it was decided that full-time school liaison officers were needed. In 1970 these officers were given the following objectives:

1. To establish working relationships between the police and the school community—children, teachers and parents.
2. On the basis of this relationship to develop activities designed to help schools to discharge their responsibility for preparing their pupils successfully to face the problems and opportunities of adult citizenship.

The word 'citizenship' recurs constantly in all police work in schools; it is a vague term which may mean all things to all men. A summary of varying definitions given by police officers might be 'the understanding of the operation of society—its needs and problems; and ways of altering its function'. This is what education is about and what one hopes children are learning both directly and indirectly throughout their school life. The police input can give another dimension and one which requires their specialist knowledge and guidance.

The Sussex police now have twenty full-time school liaison officers. They are responsible to the community relations branch staff. Every school liaison officer is left to plan his own programme but is offered help and guidance by the Headquarters staff. Some training is given by a local teacher training college, and all school liaison officers are given hints on the preparation of courses and advice on how to handle children and relationships in the schools.[1]

The recommended subject material draws heavily on the programmes drawn up by the Metropolitan Police. Most of the school liaison officers are involved in running courses in the schools as opposed to paying one-off visits which are not regarded as being particularly useful. At the end of each course, which is likely to consist of a weekly lesson, the children are given an examination. Through this sort of activity the police are able to build up good relations with both children and teachers. The Sussex police invest a great deal of manpower into their school liaison programme and they believe that this is amply justified by the fact that not only are they establishing close relationships with the citizens of tomorrow, but they also find that 60 per cent of their recruits come to them as a result of the schools programme.

Few police forces are prepared to give the same sort of commitment to school liaison, in terms of manpower, as the Sussex force. School liaison tends to be seen as part of the work of the community liaison officers or an additional commitment for the home beat officers. In London, until 1968 the Metropolitan Police confined school visits to road safety lectures. Between 1968 and 1972 the school-police contacts increased but there was no official policy. In 1972 the community liaison officers were encouraged to increase their school involvement and in 1974 this became official force policy. The community liaison inspector in each division is responsible for co-ordinating school involvement. The primary schools are allocated to the home beat officers and the secondary to the juvenile bureau officers who will have around four to eight schools each. The objective of the programme is that every class in every school should be visited at least once a year by a police officer. Police officers who are going into the schools get a four-day training course at the Roehampton Institute to help them develop skills in teaching children. A most impressive teaching kit has been produced by the Metropolitan

Police and this is supplied to every school in the police area. A senior officer explained that the value of this distribution of teaching material was that it meant they had 'a foot in the door' in every school, whether it was visited by a police officer or not.

Most of the teaching kits developed by the police in all parts of the country have resulted from joint planning between police and education authorities. A senior Scottish police officer commenting on school involvement in Dunbartonshire in the early 1970s said, 'We used to give rather disorganised talks to school leavers; we soon realised that this occasional involvement had little value and that we needed to get together with teachers and really plan a course.' The first experiment planned by teachers and police was the making of a film of a crime, which was followed by six periods during which the various ramifications of the crime were followed through. This was so successful that police and the local education authorities decided to get together and plan a full curriculum. However, at this stage, in 1974, the Chief Inspector of Constabulary established a national planning group who were given the task of producing a teaching package, 'Living with Others', for the Scottish police. This kit has been so successful that it is being produced commercially. The Scottish police see their role in schools as being advisory and they leave the actual teaching to the teachers who present the course to the children. The community involvement officer may introduce the course, or come in at some stage to deal with a particular subject, or simply come in at the end of the course for a question session. There are no specialist school liaison officers in Scotland as this work is considered to be an integral part of the community involvement branch. Every school has a liaison officer who is either an area beat officer or some other operational policeman. The school liaison work is only part of their duties. They are expected to assist the school to resolve all problems affecting school and police such as theft, vandalism, truancy and other forms of anti-social behaviour, and also to participate in other activities organised by the community involvement branch.

One of the interesting aspects of police involvement in schools is the quick realisation by the police that they needed to make a special appeal to the non-academic child. Because of this, most courses, lessons and special projects are practical in nature and are aimed specifically at the non-achiever, the child who is most at risk. Some police forces organise 'impact' weeks when they concentrate on one school for a week and bring in every possible practical aid—police dogs, cars, etc. It is considered that this concentrated attention is of particular value to the younger child and the child whose concentration is limited. Duke of Edinburgh Award schemes and various outdoor activities are part of police involvement in schools. In Scotland the first juvenile liaison officers organised summer camps for some of the children in their areas, because they considered that the experience of living together for a period was one of the best ways of helping the children to get a more positive view of policemen.

The most important aspect of any work in schools, of any presentations made by police officers to the young, is that the right type of officer is selected. Children learn far more from the way a person behaves than from what may be said. The way the material is presented, the ability to communicate with the youngsters, is of far greater importance than anything else. The wrong man or woman in school liaison work could do a lot of damage. It cannot be work for every policeman, any more than everyone in the community could be expected to cope with such a task. The great virtue of having specialist officers is that they can be carefully selected and trained. The school liaison officers in Sussex clearly get great satisfaction from their work although they admit that they can never be sure that they are really achieving anything; to judge their success or failure they feel that they will have to wait to see the children with whom they have worked grow up. This work needs enthusiasts and many policemen will find it hard to summon up enthusiasm for a job that does not show quick returns. Many policemen maintain that the real satisfaction in police work is the fact that there is an end product—someone locked up. Such satisfaction is not available in social crime prevention. If police work is based on this measure of success—and, in practice, this is too often the case—social crime prevention has not much of a future. Real success should be the absence of crime, how few people are locked up and how many children are kept outside of the judicial system. Measuring this type of success is impossible because so many other variables are involved. Community policing will have to seek other types of job satisfaction. The school liaison officers seem to have found this alternative satisfaction although the rest of the force may well not accept their role, may be critical of what they do and unsettle them. School liaison work has as many critics in the police as any other type of positive policing; too much involvement in schools is seen as impractical for the manpower situation and lacking in positive returns for the police. One senior police officer commented on a school liaison project in

Bristol: 'The officers are not policemen any more—they are more like teachers; in fact, you can't tell them from teachers—they are just part of the school and take lessons like any other teacher.' It is very questionable that involving a policeman in a school to this level has any value for the police; it is important, if not vital, that the school liaison officer does not lose touch with his operational colleagues and skills, that he does not lose his identity as a policeman. If this happens, his value to the school must be greatly undermined. The wearing of uniform in school, of course, helps both teachers, children and the policeman himself to remember this identity.

One of the most difficult problems facing schools at the present time is truancy. Like other types of potentially anti-social behaviour, truancy is an urban disease and is less common in rural areas. It tends to occur in large schools, situated in overcrowded areas of deprivation and poor housing. No agency seems to be really interested in dealing with the problem of truants; indeed, some teachers will admit that classes are too big anyway and it is a great relief when some of the difficult children fail to appear. In many areas the procedures for dealing with truants seem both clumsy and slow. By the time the attendance officers have brought the family to court a couple of times, and this may take a year or so, the child is a confirmed truant and so far behind that he is even less able to cope than before. Truants are not necessarily delinquent or stupid; they may be bored or miserable at school, they may have fallen behind in class through no fault of their own. Unfortunately, truants are very liable to become delinquent as boredom and opportunity combine. The problem presented by these children does not necessarily disappear when they can legitimately leave school—dropouts from school frequently remain unemployed, sometimes are unemployable. When it is considered that the truancy level in some urban areas is 25 per cent or even higher, it suggests that urgent measures are needed to stem the rising tide. There are some interesting experiments—free schools, special schools, intermediate treatment centres, community schools, etc. It would seem that it is not simply the truanting children that need extra attention but the educational system that is producing them. Perhaps too little attention is being paid to this aspect.

The Sussex police regard truancy as a minor problem. This is hardly surprising considering the area which they police. In the Metropolitan area, as in Strathclyde and many other urban areas, it is a very serious and increasing problem. There have been no studies of the impact of school liaison programmes on truancy rates, but some police forces have attempted direct action to deal with the problem. The police have no legal right to stop children or take them back to school or to their parents—a fact of which most children are aware. An attempt by the Strathclyde police to return children found truanting from school resulted in some complaints from parents. Nevertheless, truancy patrols have been tried in the past in many areas of Britain with some success.[2] Dramatic reductions in the number of housebreakings and car thefts by children have been reported as a result of some of the experiments. Co-operation with schools and parents was set up in most cases—a vital factor if the exercise is to be acceptable and successful. The Strathclyde police are using their contact card system as a check on truants. Any child stopped during school hours is asked his name, address and school. This is entered on the card which is forwarded to the education authorities who alert the school attendance officers to take action. This action prevents the school attendance officers feeling that their function is being usurped by the police—a complaint made in connection with some of the truancy sweeps.

In some of the first juvenile liaison experiments in Greenock and Paisley, the juvenile liaison officers regarded truants as one of their prime targets, and would even take children to school in the morning if they were on supervision to a juvenile liaison officer. The value of co-operative truancy projects involving school, social work and parents with the police is clear—taking note of the children's names and alerting the education authorities is a valuable exercise, but further involvement by the police is not only legally questionable but would also involve heavy demands on manpower which few forces could or would consider. Dealing with truants is a problem for the education authorities. The problem for the police is the crime committed by truants. The police role must be to exert every pressure on schools to take quick and effective action to deal with their truants. This is a crime prevention exercise of proven value.

No doubt police involvement in schools will continue and increase. Police involvement in speaking to teachers during training, and developing teaching kits is essential. If children are to learn the meaning of 'good citizenship', the police share of the exercise requires understanding from the teaching staff and their full co-operation. Without this, any school contacts are unlikely to be fruitful. The teacher has to prepare the children for the police input and then build on what is given for maximum effect. To do this, the teacher must himself understand the police role and have good relationships with visiting officers. As a social crime prevention exercise, school liaison work must be the most acceptable activity the police have and one which most officers can see as being of value. Proving this by some form of controlled experiment would be constructive, if difficult. It is to be hoped that such research may soon be attempted.

Notes

1. See Appendix III.
2. Research suggests that truancy patrols are less successful than police claims would suggest. See R.V.G. Clarke and K.H. Heal, 'Police Effectiveness in Dealing with Crime: Some Current British Research', *Police Journal,* vol. LII, no. 1.

7   TRAINING*

This book has dealt with a variety of experimental and well established schemes accepted by police forces as a means of preventing crime by developing closer links with the community. Some officers involved in such projects receive special training, many do not, but have to make do with their regular police training and experience. Special training tends to differentiate between the community policeman and the 'real' policeman. This would not be admitted as policy but nevertheless, it happens in fact. It is strange that the officers selected for building up closer ties with the community should become 'not real policemen' when one considers how completely dependent on the community the police are in the execution of their daily work. Indeed, few policemen would deny that without public co-operation, law enforcement would be impossible. It has been estimated, for example, that 83 per cent of the clear-up rate in most forces is due to information supplied by the public, leaving 17 per cent as a result of direct police enquiry. Even this low figure is probably an overestimate. Some police officers mention figures as low as 4-6 per cent of crimes being solved by direct police action. Without public co-operation, therefore, the work of the police would be very difficult indeed. It seems strange that the winning of this co-operation is largely left to a small elite within the force. The main snag of this policy is that the police will be seen as consisting of the 'goodies' and the 'baddies', a point that has come out repeatedly in this book. There is real conflict within the police service regarding attitudes and response to the public, and this is recognised outside the service, particularly by young people.

In a very real sense, every policeman has to be a community policeman. Does police training facilitate the development of 'community' skills? Probably the most basic and important community skill the policeman requires is the ability to communicate with the public; the ability to respond to the widely varied demands that are directed towards the police every day; to handle the madness, anger, distress and stupidity of a diversity of persons of every race, creed and social class with courtesy and understanding; and to take the heat out of difficult situations rather than aggravate them. The Metropolitan Police Year Book describes the aim of training as 'to teach a probationer the basic practice and theory of his job and to develop confidence, leadership and the ability to communicate'. This is the aim of training; how is it achieved, and indeed, does the training given in most police establishments correspond to the aim as given, and also to the needs of the job and the role that the young police officers have to play in the community? There are few people who would give a positive answer to this question; perhaps a rather typical comment was made by Edwin Brock who said that his experience of police training 'paralysed' him.[1] He felt that if he had received no training he would at least have tackled crises in an uninhibited way, but that after his period of training he needed three to four years experience before he became sufficiently confident of his ability to cope.

Superintendent Colin Moore of the Devon and Cornwall Constabulary highlights one of the basic problems of police training.

> Our training programme leads us into the narrow field of reactive policing; which as a measure of the range and quality of police work is quite misleading; since research has shown that the service role takes more of police time than the enforcement role.[2]

There can be little dispute that police training does indeed concentrate on this enforcement role—the role which is likely to require the least amount of a policeman's time and which tends to cause barriers to arise between the police and the community. As Michael Banton points out: 'Confining the police to law enforcement minimises their chances of informal exchange and contact with the community... The effectiveness of the policeman as a peace officer lies in his participation in the life of the society he polices.' In other words, to be an effective policeman the bonds with the community must be strengthened, but if the policeman fulfils the role for which he is trained he is likely to become a 'law enforcement' officer, which will increase his alienation from the community and, therefore, reduce his capacity to be an effective keeper of the peace.

Is it fair to dismiss police training as being too law enforcement oriented and failing to give young officers the necessary groundwork on which to develop their skill as policemen? As training exists at present, a positive answer seems quite reasonable. Police forces in Britain tend to vary little in the time a new recruit spends in training. The Metropolitan training at Hendon takes 15 weeks and is followed by monthly attendance at a continuation training centre during the two years probationary period. The content of training courses is also very similar for most areas. Recruits have to learn a large amount of their Instruction Book by rote, they are expected to maintain a high standard of smartness and discipline and great stress is laid on the appearance of the recruit and the neatness of his room. It sometimes seems almost impossible for any recruit to achieve the high standards that will satisfy their instructors. Many of the youngsters find this both discouraging and unnerving and it certainly contributes towards undermining their confidence in themselves.

The course is admittedly tough and the recruits are deliberately pushed around and harassed as it is believed that the tougher the course is the greater the chance that the recruit will leave the College able to withstand the pressures he will encounter on the streets. The Home Office are reported[3] to believe that the course at Hendon is the equivalent of 18 months of undergraduate study. From the sheer acquisition of rote learning this may be the case, but the important part of 18 months of study is that a youngster has a chance of maturing and this is encouraged by the slow stimulation of the learning process. Rigid discipline and unreasonable pressure will not achieve maturity in 15 weeks, indeed, it may set back the development of the process as the young person ceases to think for himself or has the confidence to make his own decisions. Most police training establishments seem to discourage young recruits from thinking for themselves. Yet, after a few weeks, the young recruit is thrown out on to the streets of various urban areas and expected to show initiative, consideration and the ability to think for himself. Many of these young recruits would echo Edwin Brock's comment 'I was terrified when I left the training school—all my confidence was gone.'

Of course, in theory the probationary constable will initially always be accompanied by an experienced officer. In practice, because of the shortages of manpower, this is rarely possible. More usually, they will have to answer calls accompanied by a slightly more experienced probationary officer or even alone, apart from their radio. Most young probationary officers find straight infringements of the law easy to deal with, but such situations are less frequent than the marital and domestic disputes, sudden deaths and similar calls for help or assistance that pour into the police stations every day. Lack of confidence and the desire to make arrests are unlikely to increase the ability of the young policeman to communicate with the many and varied persons with whom he will come into contact in such situations. When he mishandles such situations, police-public relations suffer a setback, because the community is not prepared to make allowances for youth and inexperience when it is clothed in policeman's uniform. The public cannot discriminate between the policeman who has six months service and the one who has six years. It is important that the policeman should understand and be able to apply the law—failure to do this will cause serious problems. Yet there is so much that is needed to enable him to fulfil his role and handle the daily round of problems. A good example of this is dealing with the problems of death. Recruits are carefully taught how to take a dying declaration, something which they may never have to do, but equally something which is of tremendous importance. On the other hand, they are given no training on how to break the news of a sudden death, something which they will have to do many, many times during their service. It is difficult to find a police officer who has ever had to take a dying declaration; it is equally difficult to find a police officer who has not had to break the news of a sudden death to someone.

The impression given by police training is that it is militaristic in its approach and therefore unlikely to develop the sort of police officer required by a civilian force. The problem is that discipline is vital for the police force; in situations of crisis a police officer must know his role and must respond absolutely to orders. Failure to do so may endanger both his colleagues and the general public. The weakness of the present training system seems to be that a great deal of stress is laid on the external discipline, smartness, good appearance and conformity, whereas the need for the personality to discipline itself, to develop initiative and control are ignored. If initiative is not stimulated during training, it is not going to suddenly appear on the streets. There are many situations in the streets that require discipline but initiative is equally important. Detailed quotation from the Instruction Book is rarely necessary or helpful. There are few professions that really train their students adequately for the job they have to do. A great deal of learning has to go on long after training courses are over. The police, who have one of the shortest training courses of any group, also have a job to do that is infinitely more exposed than any other, that involves the wielding of great power as compared with other professional groups and that can cause enormous problems if the job is done badly.

Most continental police forces have a training course that involves at least one year in the police college. The Swedish and Norwegian police have courses that involve training in psychology, sociology and other relevant topics. There is also practical training and, as one lecturer commented: 'We try to ensure that our young officers make their first mistakes here with us rather than on the streets.' Whether such an aim is realistic may be questioned but at least there is a chance of the recruits maturing more during a year. In addition, most senior officers in Norway have to be law graduates.

Whether a year is really necessary for ordinary police training is open to dispute; it is the process and direction of training that is of far greater importance. If the period spent under training is devoted to rigid, demanding and unimaginative exercises, if stereotyped reactions and narrow attitudes are encouraged and the community outside is categorised into 'them and us', and the recruit becomes unsure of himself, unnerved and feels isolated, the chances of his being able to develop easy and relaxed relationships with the community he has to serve would seem remote. As we keep reiterating in this book, the police are dependent on the public for the fulfilment of their role in the community.

Ragnar Hauge comments:

the maintenance of peace and order involves the public. Members of the public are both the ones who demand that peace and order shall be maintained and the ones who threaten it... If the public regard the police as hostile, unjust or incompetent, then the control of traffic and demonstrations and street patrolling and all other encounters between the police and public will be far more difficult than if the police are regarded as friendly, just and competent.[4]

Hauge goes on to describe the hostility aroused by the police in their dealings with particular groups—coloured immigrants, young people with long hair, drug takers etc., commenting that 'the conduct of the police towards different groups of people, conduct that may be derived from their attitude towards them, will, at the same time provide the basis for the attitude of the group towards the police'. He suggests that a vicious circle has developed in which 'attitudes and conduct will influence and strengthen each other both

within the police and among the public'. The problem i
break this vicious circle. Hauge suggests the use of carefully
officers for dealing with conflict situations and increasing
between the police and the community, which is indeed what ...y
police forces in Britain are attempting to do. He does not mention
training although he does stress the importance of selecting the right
men for the job. Training cannot transform a highly prejudiced,
narrow, aggressive person into a mature and controlled policeman.
If selection is failing, the job of training is that much more difficult.
It would seem that at present, training programmes are reinforcing
and developing some of the weaknesses and stereotypes that contribute to the 'vicious circle', rather than giving the new recruits a
deeper understanding of the problems of the community and the
means of developing the necessary social skills to handle these
problems. It may be useful to have specially selected and trained
officers handling certain delicate problems and situations, but it is
unrealistic to imagine that they can compensate for a police force
that is largely unprepared for policing within the community.

To return to the 'vicious circle'; if training seems to militate
against breaking it on the police side, public expectations reinforce it
on the community side. 'In most countries the traditional view holds
that the policeman's job is connected with notions of toughness and
violence. The image attracts job applicants of the same vein and
therefore is permanently confirmed by police recruiting.'[5] Few
recruits come to the job with a real understanding of the tough,
boring and frequently irritating nature of the work and the public
amongst whom they move. Even judges seem to have a distorted idea
of a policeman's role. Lord Devlin comments, in a James Smart
lecture: 'we should try to get back to the idea that the police are a
body that exist to deal with real crime'. One wonders what the
learned judge meant by 'real crime' and how he would see the police
dealing with it in isolation from the community. As has been said
before, 'real crime' is probably the least of the policeman's problems. The average day will contain innumerable incidents, domestic
rows, accidents, deaths, lost dogs, burst water pipes, drunks, fires
and so on; some days will be full, some days less so, some incidents
will uncover real crime, many will not. During one year in Manchester, 400,000 emergency calls made to the police were seeking
advice on such matters as ill fitting shoes or pregnancy testing as well
as more serious matters. The majority did not deal with crime at all.
Most of the incidents will involve contact with the public and every

contact will either bring the policeman closer to the community or the contrary. If the former is the case, then the policeman will find that it is easier to get co-operation in dealing with 'real crime' and will have made a contribution towards breaking the vicious circle which bedevils police-public relations. The former is more likely to be the case if the policeman has been adequately prepared for the job he has to do.

The training process which is started as a new recruit goes on throughout a policeman's career. Most policemen will attend special courses on promotion as well as for specialist branches such as fire-arms, CID, crime prevention, drugs, and special courses at universities and colleges. Most forces give some sort of training to their community liaison officers. In Scotland these courses tend to be local, in England there is a national course as well as the local train-ing. The value of some of these special courses is open to question as sometimes one gets the feeling that first it is decided a course is a 'good idea' and then 'how shall we fill it?' The filling is likely to be a lot of specialised lectures aimed at 'broadening' outlook. Perhaps this broadening needs a little more thought and clearer definition so that courses can be more realistically planned. Every lecture needs a positive objective and should fit with the general aim rather than being seen as part of a vaguely improving process.

In a paper on 'Training the Police in Family Crisis Intervention'[6], the authors compare two training programmes implemented in New York City by Bard (1970) and in Louisville by themselves. They found that training in family crisis intervention was not necessarily accepted or absorbed by police officers. This became evident from the New York project which at first was not particularly successful. The reasons they suggest for this are twofold. First, that most police systems reject family trouble as being a legitimate area for police involvement and secondly 'the educational level of most police forces is not particularly high and there is a traditional distaste for service functions, along with an almost single-minded orientation towards crime control'. The authors developed a training pro-gramme that was practical in orientation and, as such, was infinitely more acceptable to the police. 'When the officers saw that they were not to be tested, probed or submitted to criticism for personal beliefs or values, they soon accepted the staff and approached the training with some measure of trust and enthusiasm.'

This interesting paper demonstrates some of the main problems involved in police training. Any subject that cannot be seen as directly concerned with law and order is likely to be resisted, and may even become the subject of ridicule. When the subject is obviously aimed at changing the attitudes and behaviour of the police, it inevitably arouses anxiety among those attending and is likely to be rejected. The idea that police training should seek to change the attitudes of those involved is questionable. A police force is likely to be fairly representative of the community it serves and will therefore contain a wide range of personalities and attitudes among its officers. To believe that each recruit, each serving officer, should be hammered into the same mould is unrealistic and dangerous. If community liaison officers feel that they are being pressured into changing their attitudes and outlook, they are bound to feel defensive and resist, either openly or quietly, thereby undermining the whole aim of training. The aim of any special community liaison training should be to increase the understanding of the various problems of society and, with this increased understanding, there will develop the ability to understand and handle personal feelings and attitudes towards various social problems and minority groups. Training should not aim to make people change their attitudes and feelings, but rather enable them to acknowledge what these attitudes and feelings are and handle them in situations of stress. Everyone suffers from some sort of prejudice—it may be aroused by black skins, red hair, large hats, pickets, fur coats, regional accents, dogs, fat ladies, trade unions etc.—and a policeman will meet them all in the course of his career. He cannot love everyone, he cannot hope to overcome his own feelings of prejudice; what he has to do to become an effective community policeman is to learn to handle his prejudice, so that he is able to respond to the person who arouses it in a manner that will not alienate that section of the community which he serves. If policemen, or anyone else for that matter, are made to feel guilty or under attack because they happen to have a particular prejudice, their ability to handle the group involved will be undermined. If there is a tendency to orientate training courses towards 'changing attitudes' as opposed to 'handling attitudes', this must be a weakness in training.

Another training problem highlighted by the American research, is the practical relevance of course content to the issues confronting the police. Some community liaison training courses devote a great deal of time to the discussion of important theoretical issues. These may be of great interest and arouse discussion but, unless backed by practical examples, may be quickly forgotten. For example, in an early course run for the community involvement officers of Glasgow City Police, it was considered important to include lectures on the work of the social work department and the approved schools. There was a lot of irritation among the police officers after these sessions which they considered to have been a lot of 'waffle'. For the next course the procedure was changed. A case was allocated to each course participant and he visited the relevant social work office and spent a morning discussing the work there and his particular case. The cases chosen were all of children who had gone to approved school and visits were arranged to the relevant schools. Here the course members were able to discuss their cases as well as see the work of the school. The staff of the schools were able to explain the use of weekend leave, a very sore issue with the police, and the planning of release. At the end of the course, each participant presented his case and there was general discussion regarding the role of social work and approved schools. Setting the realities of particular cases against what was previously seen as meaningless 'waffle' enabled those involved to develop more insight into both the role of the various departments involved and the needs of the youngsters who get caught up into the system. Sadly this procedure is no longer used on courses as the problem of confidentiality has caused social work departments to withdraw their co-operation.

Problems about how to make training relevant to the job are not new and certainly not peculiar to the police service. Most professional training can be faulted for narrowness, lack of imagination and impracticality. Training tends to prepare the student for performing his job in isolation both from the needs of the recipient and the practical issues of the community. Doctors are trained to recognise disease, but their ability to recognise unhappiness and fear and the influence these have on the physical state of their patient seems inadequately developed. Social workers are given high ideals but perhaps an inadequate amount of reality. Teachers learn the theory of imparting knowledge but not the practicalities. Such comments could be made of a multitude of professions. An additional weakness of most training is that the students are given inadequate preparation for working with other professional groups, and entirely lack any real understanding of the role which other professions have to play in the community. 'Working together' is seen from each narrow standpoint, and other professions that approach problems differently are seen as being in conflict. No group attracts this label more frequently than the police; probably no group uses it more. Yet common sense must surely point to the absolute need for each group to function in its own particular way. If policemen approach the problems of law and order in the manner of social workers, society would suffer. If social workers approach the problems of the distressed and needy as the guardians of law and order, there would be little help for the suffering of many. There are situations where each role overlaps and each group needs to understand the function of the other. There are no training courses that facilitate this sort of co-operation, a co-operation that is vital if society is ever going to come to grips with the problem of anti-social behaviour.

Many people are aware of this problem and many efforts are being made to do something about it. Post-training courses, conferences, summer schools, all aim to bring together a variety of professional groups involved in dealing with the problems of anti-social behaviour. Many such gatherings have a very positive effect and open up channels of communication which increase understanding and efficiency. One such experiment was tried in 1977 by the Department of Administration at the University of Strathclyde. A series of ten weekly seminars was organised on the theme of the role of punishment in the control of anti-social behaviour, a theme likely to arouse considerable differences of view. Participants in the course amounted to 25 and involved a judge, policemen, social workers, teachers, prison governors, residential workers, psychiatrists, psychologists, reporters to the Children's Hearings and a psychiatric nurse. For the first seven seminars an outside speaker was invited to give a paper which was followed by a discussion. The last three seminars were devoted to papers from the course delegates. At the end of the course everyone involved agreed that it had been useful and interesting and had widened their horizons. Overall, the impact was very limited. There were several reasons for this: (i) those selected to attend by the various professions tended to be senior people who had been involved in their profession for many years and had developed fairly strong views; (ii) because the course was run free of charge, participants tended to regard it as an optional extra, only attending those sessions that were particularly relevant to their profession; this seriously undermined the whole object of the course—those who attended regularly gained more and showed more enthusiasm for the course; (iii) participants, because of their seniority, had many other demands on their time and this contributed to their poor attendance and made it difficult for them to prepare adequately for their own presentations. However, the limited success and interest aroused suggests that such a course had value and should be tried again, if organised somewhat differently.

A series of articles on the course was published in the *Times Educational Supplement (Scotland)*[7]; the introductory article contained the following comment:

> Efficient communication between professions would greatly assist the efforts to control and reduce the level of anti-social behaviour in the community and achieve constructive teamwork. Such co-operation is only likely to come when different professional groups really understand each other's role and accept the fact that co-operation and understanding is possible. Most people are aiming for the same end, only the means of achieving it are in dispute. Understanding what these differences are and how many of them stem from a different role is likely to improve mutual understanding and may well modify attitudes.

One of the important facts which emerged from this course was the need to organise any similar series of sessions for participants who were at an earlier stage of their professional life. In addition, a continuous residential course would be infinitely preferable as it would facilitate the development of informal contacts and discussions, which are so vital to increase mutual understanding. If all those professional groups involved in dealing with anti-social behaviour would plan such a course for their recent recruits, probably after one to two years experience, there might be a chance of increasing the impact. Such a course should be residential, lasting about two to three weeks and should involve those participating in practical projects in which mixed professional groups could share experiences. It is to be hoped that such courses may one day be accepted as part of training programmes. As one professional group in such a training course, the police would achieve a more balanced idea of the social and psychological problems in the community they serve, than is possible to convey by lectures and reading; the same would be the case for every group involved.

It is probably generally accepted that the police need to get closer to the community, that community policing has an important part to play in dealing with the problems of law and order in modern society, and that society's attitudes and moves are changing rapidly—that police training, as it stands today, is not giving the young recruits the sort of preparation they need to cope with all these changes. Victorian discipline, attitudes and ideas which persist in some measure in most police establishments, can only be a barrier to the effective functioning of the police in modern society, indeed, not only to the functioning but probably also to the recruitment of the right sort of officer. This barrier must go and training is one of the most important weapons to assist its departure. Of course, policemen must know the intricacies of the law but in modern society this is insufficient as training. New recruits need to understand the people and the institutions they are to police. The digesting of vast quantities of law cannot be avoided. It should, however, be diluted with some practical opportunities to grasp the infinite diversity of the raw material on whom this law is to be practised. A good cook needs more than a cookery book; a good policeman needs more than the instruction book. Experience is part of any skill — being sure of the legal position is vital, but knowing how to use this knowledge comes from experience built onto a solid base of practical instruction. Rigid, standardised, highly disciplined, unimaginative training will produce rigid, standardised, highly disciplined, unimaginative policemen. There is no place for such people in the modern community.

Notes

* In 1979 the Commissioner set up a Steering Committee to review training in the Metropolitan Police.

1. C.H. Rolph (ed.), *The Police and the Public* (Heinemann, 1962).

2. Cranfield, 'From Crime to Social Policies' (unpublished paper, 1978).

3. *Sunday Telegraph*, Colour Supplement, July 1978.

4. *Third Criminological Colloquium*, Council of Europe, 1978.

5. Dr Steinhilper, *Third Criminological Colloquium*, Council of Europe, 1978.

6. Driscoll, Meyer and Schanie, *Journal of Applied Behavioural Science*, 9 January 1973.

7. 23 March 1977.

8 THE FUTURE

This book has explored the various means police forces are using to get closer to the community. In doing so, perhaps we have lost sight of the fact that the police are part of the community. It sometimes seems that this fact is forgotten, not only by the community and the various agencies within it, but also by the police themselves. A policeman has a very difficult role to play in a democratic society. He must function with the approval of the community, he lives in the community but he is, at the same time, part of a disciplined service and his life is bound by the police discipline regulations. To a certain extent, these regulations remove from him some of the basic freedoms which ordinary members of the community enjoy, and subject his life to a code of behaviour which many would regard as intolerable. The armed services suffer similar constraints but their role is more clearly defined insofar as they normally expect to protect the community from external threats. The police have to protect the community from some of its own members and, at the same time, live in the community as part of it themselves. To live your life according to a particular code of discipline, amongst people not subject to such restraints, inevitably sets you apart. There are inhibitions on some relationships, some feel less free if their neighbours are police families. Even the wife and children of police officers are subject to the demands of the discipline code. It causes problems for every family when a wife, husband or child gets into trouble, runs up heavy debts, behaves in an anti-social manner. For the policeman it is likely to be more than a worry, it threatens his career.

The community makes what must seem intolerably high demands on the police. Whatever the crisis, the police are expected to cope. Crime sometimes seems the least of their problems. Strikes, pickets, fires, illness, death and all the multitudinous demands of the public, must be handled with competence and patience. They must organise help in times of the breakdown of public services or in disasters, deliver babies in emergencies, handle sudden death, look after lost children and dogs, sort out impossible traffic problems and handle

106

the many disputes that occur daily within the community. In political demonstrations they must keep the peace, regardless of who the
different parties may be and with complete impartiality. Whatever
their bias may be as members of the community, their first duty must
be to the whole and not to the part with which they may feel
sympathy.

In addition to all this the police have to cope with the attentions of
the media, for whom a policeman who misbehaves is infinitely more
interesting than the policeman who does his job with efficiency and
integrity. Handling many situations is difficult enough, whether it be
a football crowd, a political demonstration or a picketing incident.
Even with disciplined training the police are still ordinary people
and, as such, will inevitably sometimes act unwisely. Unfortunately,
the ever present media too often succeed in blowing up incidents out
of all proportion, and thus aggravate police-public relations. In
addition, a policeman who behaves discreditably can cause an extent
of damage to the reputation of the police that far outweighs his
individual action. Any individual who has had a bad experience with
the police will probably regard the whole force with suspicion.
Because of distorted press reporting, many people who have no personal experience, bad or otherwise, with the police will regard them
with distrust and suspicion. It should be added that it is only right
and proper that the failings of a service which commands so much
power over peoples' lives should always be exposed to public view.
At the same time such exposure must be fair and balanced—the community must know the good as well as the bad.

To some extent the police service must be held responsible for
some of the bad publicity which they get. Excessive secrecy even
allowing for *sub judice* cases, unreasonable anger and withdrawal
when criticised, undiplomatic handling of the press generally, do not
help. It is not easy to find the right line to take with the media and the
police are generally getting more skilled at handling this thorny
problem. Certainly it is true that the treatment given by the media to
the police and by the police to the media has not improved relations
between the police and the community.

In spite of these problems, have community policing experiments,
some of which have been described, succeeded in bridging the gap
between police and community? A definitive answer to such a question at this stage in the development of community policing would be
unwise. In Scotland, where community policing has been functioning in some areas since 1956, it is only during the past four years that

community involvement branches have really started to be effectively developed all over the country. In England, such departments are only just starting to flourish. There are few police forces in England that have community projects on the Scottish model. Indeed, the Cabinet Office report on Vandalism[1] only mentioned community projects from two police forces—Strathclyde, and Devon and Cornwall. Of course, community policing means more than community projects and many forces have developed and are developing specialist work with juveniles and their families. The idea is slowly catching on but it will take time to become really effective. In ten years or so, we may be able to make a more realistic assessment.

To attempt some sort of assessment however, it is worth considering more closely why police get involved in community policing experiments, why and if this should be different from ordinary policing—is not every policeman a community policeman and if not, why not? Apart from the general need to get closer to the community, most senior officers realise that their work as crime prevention officers, which is what all policemen must be, depends not only on the general public but also on the work of other agencies. As was shown in Chapter 5, trying to prevent the young, and the not so young, getting caught up in crime, when social conditions seemed to encourage anti-social behaviour, proved to be a losing battle. To be effective the police must co-operate with every agency in the community that has an impact on the quality of life. This sort of co-operation is beginning to work, other agencies are seeing the value of working with the police, the police are seeing the value they can gain from close co-operation with planning education, housing, social work, architects etc. In areas where there has been good co-operation, there is no doubt that the police and other agencies are working together effectively for the benefit of the community. This gap does seem to be closing in a great many places.

Community policing also fulfils the need for a specialised approach in dealing with juveniles and immigrants. How effective have the various efforts been? This is a difficult question to answer. Part of the problem is that, although it is specialised officers that will deal with the juvenile once difficulties have arisen or offences been committed, the actual day-to-day contact on the streets is with the ordinary uniformed officers whose attitude may sometimes be less than sympathetic. As has been demonstrated in this book, this can lead to a separating of the 'good' and the 'bad' policeman, something which benefits no one and makes no contribution towards the improvement of relationships with the community as a whole. Many senior officers are well aware of this problem and seek to do something about it. The Chief Constable of the Devon and Cornwall force, John Alderson, has produced a small booklet which is given to every probationary constable. In this booklet, John Alderson outlines the role of a police officer, emphasising that he must function 'not merely as a law enforcer but as a community leader'. He goes on to point out that personal prejudices must be set aside:

> It should be remembered that the police are not set up to serve the nice, competent, clean people only, but they are to serve all members of the community including the incompetent, the poor and the needy. Good police officers, therefore, accept the community they serve as their community with all its faults since they are an integral part of it.

John Alderson has given practical backing to the words he addresses to his new officers, by setting up one of the most interesting community policing experiments in the UK.

The work of specialised branches must be questioned if it is not seen as part of the pattern of policing in the area. Many officers involved in community liaison branches complain that it is not the community that give them problems but their own colleagues. The problem is that police work exposes young officers to dealing with the weakness, degradation and evil that exist in most societies. This experience will inevitably harden some, embitter others and lead many to take a very distorted view of the community. It is particularly hard on the new recruits who may have high ideals which are quickly shattered by their experiences on the street. Many probationary constables have said 'You get hard quickly—you have to if you are going to survive.' It is easy to forget this aspect of policing —an aspect which must contribute to the separation of police from the community. It is not just the community that rejects the police, the police themselves sometimes reject the community, and 'If the police regard the public as hostile they will tend to interpret their actions as motivated by hostility.'[2]

Involvement in specialised community liaison work can be a positive experience for police officers, enabling them to see some of their bad experiences in proportion. It gives many officers a chance to see another aspect of the community and increases their awareness of the complicated mechanisms that cause people to offend. It may initially make them unsure of their role when they return to ordinary police departments but, as many community liaison officers have said, once they have settled down again they feel that they have become better policemen, able to take a wider view of the problems which confront them.

One measure of the success the police have in getting closer to the community might be recruitment. It is generally believed that the low level of recruitment was due to bad pay and that now pay has been raised to a reasonable level, recruitment will improve. This is happening but I wonder if it is simply a matter of pay. If a good image is projected to the community, if the police are seen as part of the community, a positive force in the community, then surely there will be increased recruitment. If, on the other hand, the police are seen in a negative light, cut off from the community, a semi-military force, recruitment will not rise as it should. The way of life will appear 'too different' for the youngsters who might be interested. It is not just a matter of caring about law and order, it is also a matter of understanding the process of doing something about the problem. If the action that is taken appears very negative, if the police are seen in an unfriendly way by the community, the idea of becoming a policeman will be that much less attractive. Sussex police say they get 60 per cent of their recruits through the school liaison programme; that is, through the youngsters coming to understand the policeman as a person. This is a two way process—the public need the opportunity to get to know their police force, and the police need to get closer to the public so that this understanding may be achieved.

Some people believe that community policing should be developed far beyond the present level of effort. Henri Ferraud[3] suggests that a special preventive police force should be established, taking on activities that have not been considered before. He suggests that the preventive police should undertake the socialisation and education of the young by the establishment of 'prevention' clubs and leisure centres, where young people could learn practical and sporting skills, car and motor bike driving and repair for example; in addition, youth information and guidance centres, medico-social centres for drug addicts, centres for those in moral danger and lectures to schools should be part of the role of the preventive police. He does add: 'We are well aware that our plan is ambitious and may even appear to some as over ambitious.'

Even accepting that crime is not an isolated phenomenon and that to deal with it effectively, to prevent its occurrence, one needs to give attention to the environment in which crime flourishes and to the factors which increase the chances of the young offending, the idea of the police carrying the role of prevention to the level M. Feraud suggests would seem unrealistic and perhaps even dangerous. The discussion stimulated by M. Feraud's paper brings out the feeling of the risks inherent in over involvement by the police in dealing with potential offenders, risks of victimisation, of trespassing on the territory of other services etc. Some of these risks are averted if the police role with the potential offender is brief and practical, and complicated cases are handed over to other agencies. M. Feraud's interesting paper stimulates the thought that perhaps policing has turned a full circle. In the early 1900s it was the police who started the first 'probation type service' in Glasgow,[4] followed later in London where eventually there developed the 'court missionary' who became the probation officer of today. Perhaps the new community liaison departments are starting something similar? Perhaps one of the spin-offs from community liaison branches may be a renewed appreciation of the importance of a probation-social work input that is closely associated with the police service, intervening on request of the police in situations that require preventive care as opposed to aftercare. To a very limited extent the Douglas Inch Centre for Forensic Psychiatry in Glasgow has attempted to work with the police in this way. Police officers who have become aware of youngsters at risk have referred them to the centre for help, and in some cases continue working with the Centre and the youngster. In this way some young people and their families, who might not otherwise receive help, have come to the Centre and have received support which has, in some cases, prevented further problems developing.[5]

The question recurs—is it either necessary or useful to have specialised community liaison branches? Such specialisation does have risks attached, particularly if there is a lack of understanding regarding the role of such a branch. In many forces one hears the complaint that the senior officers do not seem to realise what the community liaison branch is about, and tend to use it as a dumping ground for difficult jobs that no one wants to do and for whom there is no obvious candidate. This is particularly true when it comes to problems that involve contact with the public; because the community liaison branch is seen as specialising in public relations it is expected to undertake most of these tasks. This policy has dangers because it tends to emphasis the 'good' and the 'bad' policeman idea—if it is always the community liaison officers who speak at meetings and attend conferences, both the public and the police are going to suffer. On the one hand, the public suffer because they will tend to say, as has happened 'Inspector Brown is not a real policeman—he's a community liaison officer. I wish the others were like him.' The sad thing about such a statement is that the others probably are like Inspector Brown; its just that they and the public never get a chance to find out. On the other side, of course, it means that the 'other policemen' are cut off from this very valuable 'reality testing' with the public and can continue to work in isolation from the mellowing contact with the community. There is also the additional temptation, which some forces find irresistible, to use the specialised branch solely in a public relations role. Such activities as concert parties, old peoples' outings, sports days and the sort of activities which attract the Press but do little to improve community contacts with the difficult groups, who never attend such functions anyway, are thrust on them. Community liaison departments have a real job to do and need to be encouraged and supported in this job, not inundated with a multiplicity of demanding but unrewarding public relations exercises.

An additional problem is that specialised branches may encourage the rest of the force to feel that they can handle the public and even the sensitive groups within the community in any way they like, and the community liaison officers will make it all right if there is trouble. It may even encourage the force to feel that they have to be particularly tough on some special problem groups to compensate for their 'soft' colleagues, who, by their attitudes are 'encouraging anti-social behaviour'. There are many individual police officers whose relationships with, and understanding of, the young and the immigrant population are excellent; who are able to communicate with all sections of the public in a useful and positive way. Unfortunately there are also officers who have little understanding and less patience with problem groups and whose actions seriously undermine the image of the police and the work of the specialised branches. This is a problem which needs attention. Every policeman must be a community policeman; he must understand the needs and problems of sensitive groups and difficult areas. His failure cannot be excused or dismissed because he is a good thief catcher. He may catch criminals—his actions could also create a few. A policeman, because of his uniform and authority, the power he has in the community can, by unwise handling of the young and the immigrant, set up anti-authority and anti-social reactions, which can have far-reaching consequences. Conversely, sensitive and understanding handling of problem groups and difficult areas, can have a far more positive impact than many police officers seem to realise.

Some senior officers are on record as saying they will not have specialised community liaison officers because all their men are community officers. This seems a very laudable attitude, if it is genuine and not just a way of doing nothing and allowing the force to detach itself from the community. It makes sense to put pressure on a force and ensure that all the officers react in a constructive and sympathetic way to the varied people and demands that present themselves each day. The problem of the 'good' and the 'bad' policeman would not arise in such circumstances, and there must be much greater pressure on every rank.

It is difficult to see that any force can, in realistic terms, manage without a specialised branch. The legislation for children and young people alone means the establishing of much closer contacts with social workers and education, contacts which are dependent on personal relationships to encourage trust and co-operation. If there was no specialised officer dealing with such problems, if someone different appeared each time, effective working contacts would be difficult. In addition, just as the CID, Fraud Squad, Drug Squad and other officers learn to know the people and problems, the areas most at risk, the situations where they must be most vigilant, so the community liaison officer, if he is allowed, develops similar skills and understanding. The important point is that senior officers allow these skills to contribute to policing in their area; that the community liaison officer is really allowed to do his job, to influence policing in his patch, to advise and be sure his advice is heeded. Too often, advice is sought too late or is ignored. The only conclusion one can draw from such incidents is that community liaison is seen as an optional extra, a public relations exercise or a soothing syrup to be applied on to damage created by unwise action. Of course, every specialist branch in the police suffers from the feeling that sometimes their activities are undermined by their colleagues in other branches but community liaison, because of the nature of the role it has to play, seems to suffer most. The responsibility for this must lie at the door of senior officers who fail to appreciate what community liaison is about and do not give the officers involved the sort of backing they need to do their job effectively. Until the senior ranks in the police service both understand and accept the philosophy of community policing, the job of the community liaison officers will always be difficult and, in the eyes of the community, unconvincing: 'The police are not really interested in ordinary people —they are just putting on an act.' Unfortunately, many people believe this and the actions of some senior officers only serve to reinforce this feeling.

Throughout this book there have been references to the Council of Europe *Third Criminological Colloquium* on 'The Police and the Prevention of Crime'.[6] One of the main objectives of this colloquium was to review various aspects of preventive policing, and the relationship of police with community. The importance of this was pinpointed by the Chairman, Mr S. Donmezer, in his opening address:

> In modern cities there was no longer the informal control that once used to be exercised by neighbours. Consequently, it was necessary to increase the official control exercised by the police. Furthermore the treatment of offenders did not often produce positive results. For this reason, it was expedient to set up preventive measures.

This statement underlines the fallacy of the philosophy held by some policemen that they are fulfilling their role in preventing crime, as laid down in 1829, by catching villains and having them locked up. As Mr Donmezer said, in modern urban society this does not work. Prevention is better than cure and prevention does not mean catching after but rather catching before.

At the conclusion of the colloquium, Michael Banton produced a list of conclusions[7] which were discussed by the delegates. All the conclusions were not generally accepted except as a basis for further discussion. One of the criticisms made of the conclusions was that they were too close to the British conception of policing—a criticism which was questioned by other delegates. The important point was made that it is unwise, in any police force in any country, to draw a sharp distinction between repressive and preventive activities—a point that is worth keeping in mind when considering the role of specialist departments dealing with community liaison.

In general the discussions at this international gathering indicate the increasing awareness of governments that policing modern, urban, democratic societies can only be achieved effectively if the police and the community work together. Imposing repressive measures on the community will only increase the gap between the police and the people they serve. How one can achieve a satisfactory and acceptable form of policing is still an unresolved question. The colloquium notes, in the closing paragraph of its report: 'In conclusion, it may be mentioned that some participants were concerned about the difficulty of arriving at any generally acceptable understanding of the police as a social institution.'

Any discussion of the police as a social institution tends to involve some nostalgic references to the 'village bobby'. As has already been suggested, juvenile liaison could be seen as an attempt to recreate the village bobby in urban areas. The legislation for children—Social Work (Scotland) Act and the Children and Young Persons Act—could be seen as attempts to recreate the community pressure and concern that existed in rural society for the young offenders in their midst. Is it useful to attempt such exercises in modern society—what relevance has the village bobby, the caring community, to the deprived communities in western Scotland, the coloured communities of London, Birmingham and many other urban conurbations? Can we hope to graft on historic institutions that were concerned with a different way of life, a different set of values? Indeed, was there really ever a village bobby, a concerned community in the urban 'stews'—was there really a gloriously crime-free society such as one tends to imagine. However one answers this question, one thing is certain —looking backwards is not going to help solve the problems of the future. Grafting on manmade legislation in the hopes of stimulating feelings of responsibility and concern may well set up the same sort of rejection as doctors found when attempting to graft human organs. When the body rejects the organs, the individual dies. Legislation that is forced upon communities, without sufficient attention being given to the processes of rejection, may have a very destructive effect. We do not know how to prevent crime, we do not know how to cure offenders, we do not know the most effective way for the police to function in the community, we cannot even agree how these problems should be investigated. To return to the last sentence of the Council of Europe report:

It was suggested that a survey of the legal framework of police activity in European countries might facilitate discussion at any future Council of Europe conferences concerning the police, but lawyers and sociologists would probably have different ideas about the best way in which to design any such enquiry.

One might add that the police and the community would probably disagree with both! Such disagreement should not necessarily be regarded as depressing—at least there is an awareness of the need for action, a realisation that all is not well, that preventive policing and community responsibility are essential elements in the fight against crime. So long as this awareness exists and discussion and research continue, there is hope that positive change will eventually be effected, and in such a way that the community as a whole—and that includes the police—will accept it.

In spite of the problems and difficulties that have been described in this book, there is no doubt but that, during the past decade, there has been a movement by the police and that movement has started the process of establishing closer links with the community. There are difficulties on the police side, there are weaknesses in attitudes and behaviour, but one is bound to record that it is the police who have themselves seen the need for, and initiated, this movement for change; it is the police who have taken the lead in developing co-operative ventures in communities, it is the police who have recognised the need for more realistic co-operation in all spheres. Perhaps if education, social work and maybe housing departments had shown similar awareness and movement, and if the community responded with similar movement, the gap that exists might be closed more quickly. All the effort cannot be on one side. The police in the UK have, over the past decade, made tremendous efforts to co-ordinate their role with others—sometimes the failure to reciprocate can cause reactions of withdrawal which will only set back the process of co-operation. No one, in modern society, can function in an ivory tower—social workers cannot hope to help their clients effectively without the co-operation of other parts of the community, teachers cannot hope to educate their charges without involving the wider issues implicit in good citizenship, policemen know that they can never hope to prevent crime without the help and support of the community of which they are a part. It is exciting to see the effect of this awareness on the British police and the immediate and constructive efforts that they are making to respond. These efforts can do nothing but good for the public image of the police force in Britain.

Notes

1. HMSO, 1978.
2. R. Hauge, 'The police and the Prevention of Crime', *Third Criminological Colloquium,* Council of Europe, 1978.

3. H. Ferraud, 'The Police and the Prevention of Crime', *Third Criminological Colloquium,* Council of Europe, 1978.

4. D. Grant, *The Thin Blue Line* (Long, 1973), p.54.

5. See Appendix I.

6. Strasbourg Conference, 1977.

7. See Appendix IV.

Appendix I : Case Histories

To illustrate the work of the juvenile liaison officers and the community involvement officers I have collected some case histories. These may read like success stories—most juvenile liaison officers and community involvement officers will readily admit that as well as successes there are many failures. However, it seemed sensible to use those cases where the outcome was successful to illustrate some of the ways in which intervention by the police can be constructive, and does not trespass on the work of other agencies, but rather backs them up. No case is ever taken on by the police without first ensuring that other agencies, such as social work departments, have no prior involvement. Indeed, no offender is even cautioned without prior consultation with social work agencies.

It is interesting how often in these case histories, the families use the limited support the police give them to cope practically with minor family problems which might easily develop into more serious situations. The feeling that there is an authority figure helping, as opposed to criticising, seems to enable some inadequate parents to cope with the problems of their families in a more effective way.

Laurie (aged 15 years)

Laurie lived with his mother in a corporation house. They were hard up but the house was clean and tidy. Laurie's mother contacted the police and asked for help with her son as he was constantly changing his job and stealing money from the home. A juvenile liaison officer contacted Laurie who was initially very wary of the police. The juvenile liaison officer gradually established a good relationship with Laurie and discovered that the boy had wanted to go into the RAF but had failed the exam. This experience had contributed to his present unsettled behaviour. The juvenile liaison officer contacted the RAF and found that, in fact, Laurie had only failed in mathematics. A resit of the exam was arranged and the boy worked hard in preparation for it. He was successful but there were some further delays. The RAF said they could not take him for nine months. The juvenile liaison officer persuaded them to speed up the boy's admission and, in fact, Laurie was called for after one month. His ensuing career with the RAF was highly successful. The juvenile liaison officer maintained a friendly contact with Laurie for about nine months. His contact was that of guide and helper and he visited the boy and his mother about nine or ten times. The police intervention at a critical stage might well have been the vital factor which prevented Laurie getting caught up in serious crime.

Charles (aged 12 years)

Charles was taken on for supervision after a minor theft. He and his mother and very young twins lived in a single room in a very poor area. His mother was awaiting her divorce from the father. Cooking was over a primus stove and the other occupiers of the house were well known to the police. Drunken couples would crash into the room at all hours of the night. The police fitted a bolt to the door to keep out intruders. The corporation were threatening to put the family on the streets because of overcrowding. The juvenile liaison officer realised that this family presented a serious social problem and, as was usual in such cases, he sought the advice of the social work department. The social work department asked the juvenile liaison officer to continue to handle the case as there was so much difficulty and trouble in the environment around the family, and it seemed more appropriate for the police to be involved. In addition, it was felt that the police might have more influence on the corporation to get the family rehoused. After some months, the juvenile liaison officer succeeded in getting the family rehoused and there was a marked improvement in their life style. Charles had not got into any further trouble and the juvenile liaison officer decided to take the boy on a three week experimental adventure training course.

Supervision in this case lasted for fourteen months. The juvenile liaison officer continued to handle it in spite of the problems presented, because the social work department felt it appropriate. The practical involvement of the police, combined with the sympathetic interest shown in Charles, had the necessary impact and 2½ years later Charles has still not reoffended.

Anthony (aged 7 years)

Anthony lived in poor circumstances in a corporation house with his father and cohabitee and several children of mixed parentage—two being Anthony's siblings, two being children of his father and cohabitee, and one being the illegitimate son of the cohabitee. Anthony was referred by his headteacher after the boy had been caught stealing money from a teacher's handbag. His behaviour at school was not good. The juvenile liaison officer made enquiries at the home and found that, as well as very poor social conditions, there were indications that Anthony was suffering from some mental disorder. Neither the boy's father nor the woman appeared to have any feeling for him and told strange stories regarding his bizarre behaviour. Instances were related which showed that the boy had stolen food and concealed it, although there was no lack of food in the house. He had picked holes in the wall, cut the toes out of a new pair of wellington boots and chewed holes in a new jersey. He had a habit of tying knots in shoe laces and then cutting them up into small pieces. Although some of these stories may have been exaggerated, it did seem that Anthony was a very disturbed boy. In view of this, the juvenile liaison officer sought the advice of the child guidance clinic and the family doctor. As a result of discussions, the boy was referred to a psychiatric clinic and thence to a psychiatric hospital. In this case the juvenile liaison officer acted as a linkman, identifying a problem and referring the child to the agency that was most likely to benefit him.

Frances (aged 14 years)

Frances was the middle girl in a family of five. Her parents were divorced and she lived with her mother who was well known to the police and has several convictions for serious assault and breach of the peace. The eldest boy in the family had a formidable record, mainly for violence. In spite of her criminal record, the mother kept her home immaculate. Frances came to the notice of the police for shoplifting and her mother agreed to juvenile liaison officer supervision. The policewoman juvenile liaison officer found that the whole family needed help. Frances was a persistent truant. However, her mother wanted Frances to do well at school and was very co-operative. The interest in the family shown by the police seemed to help the mother who started to show more confidence in dealing sensibly with her problem. Frances joined a youth club run by a male juvenile liaison officer and was given extra attention there. Her progress at school improved and there is a chance that she may be able to take 'O' levels. She has done very well in the club, assists in the canteen and can be trusted with money.

Frances was supervised for five months, appears to have settled down and is leading a normal life. Since their first contact with the juvenile liaison officer, no member of the family has reoffended. It is hoped this pattern may continue.

John (aged 4 years)

John was referred to this office by his mother who complained that the child was difficult to handle and was outside her control. On the first visit the juvenile liaison officer found a very bright and talkative four-year-old child. The parents reported that John was abnormally violent with everyone; slept poorly, i.e. went to bed late and rose very early; had no set interest except with cars and car keys; both parents felt that he was a potential delinquent and they had failed to beat this out of him. The mother stated that she had been attending her doctor who had prescribed valium. The home circumstances were pleasant—a new house on a new estate, with the house well kept, clean and tidy. There were another two children in the family aged three years and eight years; mother is a housewife and father manages a butcher shop.

As a result of this visit, the juvenile liaison officer decided to contact a psychiatric clinic. A psychologist went with him on his next visit to the home and, as a result, John was referred to a child psychiatrist. As this child had a high intelligence and had missed the school entrance by only thirteen days, it seemed as though the solution would be simple and that the child would be admitted to primary school. However, this was not to be as John had to wait until the next intake at his school, during which time he attended the child psychiatrist with his mother. This child has not come to the notice of the police since.

Theft by Housebreaking by a Child

This concerns a youth who, in December 1977—when 14 years of age—was detected and subsequently charged with theft by housebreaking.

Enquiry was made and his home circumstances were particularly good, both parents being of professional class.

The boy was a 'first offender' and indeed had never come to the attention of the police previously. He was, therefore, considered suitable for a police warning and this was carried out in the presence of his mother at a police office.

The subject and parent readily agreed for the youth to be supervised by a police officer and, when this was implemented, a good relationship was formed between the police, parent and boy.

The youth accepted an invitation to go to an outdoor centre where—along with others—he resided for a week and was supervised by police community involvement branch officers on outdoor and social activities.

This week was thoroughly enjoyed by the boy and, though after his return the supervision was terminated, he has not—after a year —caused any concern to his parents or come to the notice of the police.

Rory (14 years) and Neil (13 years)

The boys are brothers and there are another three older brothers and two younger sisters in the family. They reside in a four-apartment corporation house in a large borough. It is situated in a part of town which is designated as an area of multiple deprivation.

The family appears to have a history of violence with one older brother having been convicted of attempted murder.

The father, who is an alcoholic, and has a psychiatric history, has been married twice and his present wife does her best for the step-children. Unfortunately, she appears to have somewhat limited intelligence and does not know how to handle either Rory or Neil.

Rory came to the notice of the CIB when he assaulted another boy and stole from him, and a few months later Neil came to the attention of the CIB when he assaulted his stepmother. Both were formally warned and their cases were considered suitable for supervision.

On his first visit to the home the CIB officer was pleasantly surprised with the appearance and cleanliness of the home. Communications were difficult because of the father's alcohol problem and the stepmother's position and low intelligence. It appeared that whenever a crisis situation arose in the home, the father turned to alcohol and was unable to support his wife in her handling of the boys. After a number of visits by the CIB officer he learned that Rory's behaviour had been so erratic at school that he had been referred to the educational psychologist. Evidently, Rory thought that if he was 'bad enough' he would be removed from his own home and placed in the pleasant surroundings of a children's home.

During one of his visits, the CIB officer learned that both boys were 'bed-wetters' and as Rory's conduct in the home seemed to improve, so Neil seemed to go from bad to worse.

As a result of the CIB contact with the school, both boys were sent to an assessment centre and the grandmother moved in to assist the stepmother, whose general health was beginning to deteriorate to such an extent that she was admitted to hospital suffering from a heart attack.

About this time, the CIB officer was visiting the home regularly and was in touch with the social work department. The father, with the encouragement of the various pressures on him, began to cope in the home and the stepmother's health improved gradually until she returned home.

With the assistance of the CIB officer, a holiday was arranged for the boys through the social work department, to give the stepmother a chance to regain some of her strength to enable her to cope with the boys on their return.

The father then appreciated that he had a problem with alcohol and was put in touch with Alcoholics Anonymous.

Relationships with the family improved and the bed-wetting reduced. Neil still had the occasional flare-up, when the CIB officer would be called in by the parents.

The family appeared to settle down, the house was decorated and the garden was restored, mainly by the boys who eventually found employment with Community Industry.

Supervision in this case was more than normal, 33 visits over a period of two years.

This case portrays an excellent example of co-operation between the CIB and the statutory agencies, social work and education departments.

The relationship which the CIB officer was able to forge with this family, was undoubtedly a lifeline for each member of the family who was going through a stormy passage at that time.

A Case of Glue-sniffing

This concerns a youth—born 15 March 1964—who came to the notice of the police for solvent abuse and truancy. The boy was from a working-class home with responsible parents.

In September 1978 he returned to his home smelling of, and obviously suffering from, the effects of inhalation of glue. The boy's father was extremely concerned and after consulting the family doctor was advised to take him to a child psychiatrist.

In addition to taking his son to the psychiatrist, the father learned, when contacting the head of guidance at his school, that his son was truanting and his scholastic performance had deteriorated.

A week later, the father contacted the police community involvement branch and an officer agreed to supervise the youth and make frequent calls at his home.

For almost six weeks thereafter, though the youth made regular visits to the psychiatrist and was visited by the police, he had a number of lapses when he would again indulge in 'sniffing'. When questioned as to the reason for the lapse, he would explain that he 'missed seeing the beautiful colours'.

On 1 November 1978, a case conference was held within the school and this was attended by the register teacher, guidance teacher, psychiatrist and police. The general conclusion reached —after lengthy discussion—was that, though there had been disappointment felt all round at his lapses, he should be given another chance.

The boy's conduct was satisfactory for a while after this but, on 10 December 1978, his father found him again showing the signs of solvent abuse.

The CIO attended the house and, accompanied by his father, took the subject to hospital where he was detained overnight.

After discharge, although he improved and his appointments with the psychiatrist were terminated from 18 January 1979, the other agencies continued to display an interest in the youth and, at time of submission—March 1979—he has not deviated.

The boy's father was particularly grateful for the time devoted by the police community involvement branch and it is of interest, perhaps, to note that the youth concerned has maintained contact with his youth advisory officer and indeed assists him in any project he initiates to combat glue-sniffing.

Geoffrey (aged 12 years)

Geoff came to the notice of the police when he was involved in a minor case of theft by housebreaking.

He was given a formal police warning and the case was considered suitable to be dealt with under the Youth Advisory Service. The case was allocated for supervision by a unit beat officer. Geoff is a member of a large family, consisting of his mother, three older brothers, two younger sisters and two ycunger brothers—a total of eight children between the ages of 19 and 2. His father is deceased. The family reside in a four-apartment corporation house (in an undesirable area) of a large borough. Their income is solely from public funds and money is tight.

On the constable's first visit he was not impressed by the cleanliness of the home and formed the opinion the children were poorly clothed.

This visit was during the summer months and Geoff's leisure pursuits were all out of doors. From time to time, Geoff met and spoke to the constable during his tours of duty, and assured him that he intended staying out of trouble in the future.

On a subsequent home visit, the constable learned that Geoff had failed to return to school after the summer holidays. Eventually he told the constable that he was afraid to return to school because boys were making a fool of him. Geoff at this time appeared nervous and the constable noted that the boy's attitude had changed.

Geoff's older brother thought that the other pupils would be making life tough for the boy because he was not 'as well dressed as they were in their school uniform'. Needless to say his mother was unable to afford school uniform.

The constable instructed Geoff's mother to write a note to the school detailing the circumstances of his absence and he was told to return to school.

The constable visited the school and learned that Geoff had failed to appear and also learned that he had a very poor attendance record.

The constable and the school contacted the social work department who agreed to assist, and Geoff was brought to school on the following day by a social worker. These events led to Geoff attending an assessment centre for one week in an effort to resolve the problem.

This case was then referred to the social work department who were fully aware of the problems in this family.

The supervision in this instance was carried out by a uniformed resident beat constable who, once he became aware of the problem, acted correctly and speedily to assure that the situation did not become more difficult and so create additional problems.

Peter (13 years old)

Peter first came to the notice of the police on a charge of stealing a bicycle from a shopping centre. His parents were unaware of what had happened, although Peter had retained the bicycle for two days. The boy admitted the theft and was warned at the police office. The family agreed to supervision by the community involvement branch.

Both parents were working and there appeared to be a lack of contact between them and Peter. The first visit to the home went well, in spite of the parents' apprehension regarding the police role. There was a frank and useful discussion which resulted in the parents becoming aware of their failure to show enough interest in Peter. On the next visit two weeks later, the community involvement officer found that Peter and his father had built a bicycle from scratch and were now planning to build a sledge. As a result of the interest being shown, the other members of the family became involved. One of Peter's elder brothers expressed an interest in joining the police and has since made application.

As the family seemed to be coping very well, supervision was terminated. The family have agreed to contact the police if they need any further help.

Ruth (aged 14 years)

Ruth's mother asked for police help in dealing with her daughter whom she had caught selling tickets for a fictitious raffle. There was no formal complaint but Ruth admitted the offence. She and her mother were interviewed in the police office.

Ruth's father had died suddenly seven months before, and her mother felt Ruth had changed since then. She had been writing letters to her friends and relatives and then hiding the letters in such a way that her mother would find them. The letters were fantasies containing occasional erotic passages. Ruth was also found to have a knife under her pillow. According to her mother she was prone to hanging around with a crowd of boys who were often in trouble. In addition, Ruth's attendance at school was very irregular.

Ruth visited the police station but refused to talk to the community involvement officer. A call at her home produced no better results. At this point, it was decided, subject to the mother's approval, to seek help from a psychiatric clinic. A home visit by the community involvement officer and a psychologist was arranged, but Ruth was as silent as usual. She appeared very depressed so it was decided to refer her to the clinic for treatment. Police supervision was terminated at this stage.

Ruth was not very co-operative in attending the clinic and it was decided that she required in-patient treatment and was accordingly transferred to another clinic offering such facilities. She has made some progress and the doctors feel that there is a good chance of treatment being effective.

Jane (aged 14 years)

Jane received a police warning for theft and thereafter agreed to supervision. She had a troubled background; her relationship with her mother was very poor; she was a very strong willed and stubborn girl, had been involved in solvent abuse and, finally, tended to disappear from home from time to time without warning or explanation.

The community involvement officer supervised Jane for ten months. During the early visits, Jane often failed to appear at home. After three months of supervision, these disappearances from home were persisting and causing much distress to the family. In addition, Jane had started to visit her sister who lived some distance away. While staying there, she always behaved very well.

Gradually, Jane began to improve at home and respond to the visits of the CIO. Her school work was good and she decided to try to become a children's nurse.

The CIO felt that success had really been achieved with Jane when, at a disco run by the police, she had a long conversation with her supervising officer in the presence of a group of her friends, something which would have been unthinkable a few months previously.

Pat (aged 14 years)

This case was referred to the office by the parents as Pat was keeping late hours and undesirable company.

Pat was the only daughter and youngest of a family of three. She came from a clean and tidy home.

When interviewed, her mother was very pleasant to the CIO but when speaking to or in front of Pat, she became very offhand.

Pat was also a truant from school, although it was learned at the school that she was an 'A' grade pupil and that if she took up her studies again, she could easily go on to university.

Pat was keeping company with 16-year-old girls who had officially left shcool but were not as yet working. Through them she had met a boy aged 17 years, and she would not believe it when told that the boy was well known to the police. The CIO was finally forced to tell her to check among her mutual friends and she would find at least one girl who was pregnant by him. This started her thinking but she would still not give in.

Pat stayed away from home overnight but telephoned the police office in the morning to seek assistance. She told the CIO where she was and he went and collected her. After a long discussion, Pat tried to make out that her father would not like the CIO or talk to him. They returned to her home as the CIO had arranged to meet her father there. He was most helpful and talkative and tried to give Pat every help that he could. Her father worked long hours but he was prepared to collect Pat from the Sports Centre or any other function that she wished to attend—this did not suit Pat however, as she felt she should be free to come home by herself. Pat assured the CIO that she did not wish to leave home.

Since Pat was adamant that she was going to continue keeping her present company, the CIO advised both her parents to write a letter to the Reporter to the Children's Panel stating that Pat was outside of control.

They did write the letter and both signed. Pat then asked for one more chance and her parents agreed to this. Pat has returned to school and, at the last check, had started wearing her school uniform again. She now keeps good company and has caught up with her studies. She has not been in trouble since.

Report on the Referrals Made Under Befriending (Aunts and Uncles) Scheme

1.   Susan, aged eleven years, was cautioned for theft by the bureau. Her brother, who had implicated her in the theft of £60 from the parents, was sent to court on a different matter and became the subject of a care order. The brother's appearance and subsequent placing in care had a very bad effect on the girl, due to the very close relationship between the two. Truancy from school began and her over-all behaviour pattern within the home began to deteriorate.

      Action Taken: The girl was introduced to a befriender, who is a teacher with maladjusted children in the area. The girl's behaviour improved, her truancy stopped and she has responded to family influence. Having relatives in the befriender's area, she calls at the befriender's house about every two weeks. Described by the befriender as a 'chatterbox', the link is continuing.

2.   Martin, aged 13, had, with a friend, been involved in shop-lifting, and had been cautioned for this offence. A member

of a one parent family, the mother is employed full-time in a solicitor's office, and has a strong personality. Although intelligent and studious, the boy had no real interests outside the home. The mother expressed great concern about her son and desired he should be found an outside interests.

Action Taken: A link was established to a male befriender, who had an allied interest in conservation, particularly wild birds. The boy has been encouraged to participate in a group conservation project, with the result that not only the boy, but his mother, are now actively participating in the group. The link is being maintained and the mother, boy and befriender are pleased with the situation.

3. Christopher, aged eleven, was involved with two others in burglary, for which he was cautioned. The other two older youths, both of whom were the subject of previous bureau referrals, were placed before the court. In addition, an elder brother of Christopher's, aged 15, had previously been convicted of burglary. The subject was below average at school, though with no truancy problem. His parents were most anxious that he should not follow in his brother's footsteps and it was also desirable to sever his association with the other boys mentioned.

Action Taken: A link was established with a befriender who had a good local knowledge of informal activities. An interest was gradually established in swimming and from this, inclusion in a swimming club followed. The informal contact has been maintained and both parents and befriender now indicate a greater interest by the subject in his performance at school. The befriender dealing with Christopher is in fact a link organiser within this scheme.

4. Lee, aged eleven, was cautioned for theft of an ignition key, which he had thrown away. With three brothers, one older and two younger, the parents having just separated, Lee had already been cautioned at the age of ten years for burglary. The nature of the second offence was such that it was felt, with the parents' co-operation, that positive action could be taken. This proved very difficult as the subject had no external interests at all, apart from scale model motor cars. The mother, who resides on the twentieth floor of a high rise block of flats, would not allow the subject

out once he had come home from school, as she wished to keep him under strict parental control.

Action Taken: Lee was introduced to a female befriender but initially little progress was made. Subsequently, however, the elder brother was introduced to a karate group with the result that the subject also showed an interest and this has been maintained. Indeed, the befriender, who is also a link organiser within the scheme, has persuaded the mother to assist with the catering at the karate group. The subject's school attendance, which was mediocre, has also improved.

The befriender reports that at present she is pleased with the progress made and hopes to retain the link which has been established. It has been appreciated by all concerned, however, that this has proved a difficult referral.

5.   Anthony, aged 15, was involved with two others, one an adult, in taking and driving away a motor van. The adult and the other juvenile (a persistent offender) were both charged; Anthony was cautioned. There had been no previous referral.

The parents were very concerned with the associations that this subject was maintaining and, further, that they were having difficulty in maintaining discipline within the home. The subject is an only child.

Action Taken: Anthony was introduced to a male befriender, who had an interest in golf, which was a sport also of interest to the subject. Subsequently an allied interest in art was established, with the result that the subject now has a wider variety of interests, as well as a new circle of friends. The link had been maintained, the parents having expressed their gratitude for the befriender's assistance.

6.   Trevor, aged 14, was cautioned for taking a 'dumper' truck from a building site. He is one of seven children in a family where the parents are separated. No problems were experienced at school, but the mother was finding it difficult to manage and she was concerned that the subject would start committing further offences.

Action Taken: Introduced to a male befriender, the subject has subsequently been introduced to the befriender's family. The link has been maintained, with activities taking place with the befriender's family.

7. & 8. David aged twelve was reported, with a friend aged eleven, for shoplifting (two cases), for which both youths were cautioned. An only child, his parents admit that he was spoilt. Both felt that some guidance and assistance was required.

Action Taken: Introduced to a male befriender, a rapport was quickly established, with a common interest in stamp collecting and music. The link is now a firm one and this befriender reports that he really feels like an uncle to the family. Such has been the response that the other youth concerned, Darren (aged eleven), has been placed with the same befriender, at the request of Darren's parents. Although this subject has a younger brother and sister, he is a close friend and classmate of David, and all concerned are happy with these arrangements. There are no school attendance problems in either case.

9. Steven, aged 14, was cautioned for discharging a firework in a public place. Although a minor offence, concern was expressed by the father that the boy, the oldest of three, who had no external interests, was beginning to present behavioural problems within the home. The father was divorced and admitted that the raising of the family was causing stress to the unit as a whole. Minor 'odd day' truancy was taking place.

Action Taken: Steven was introduced to a male befriender. Initial difficulty was experienced in finding suitable interests outside the home. However, the presence of rabbits, goldfish, etc. within the family home, was sufficient to establish a link, the befriender drawing on the experience of his youth in this respect. The link has been maintained, the subject now expressing an interest in sport in general, of which the befriender has a good all-round knowledge. The befriender reports that the subject is more stable, the family unit happier, with no problems at school. It is hoped that it will be possible to place the subject in a youth club in the near future.

Appendix II

JUVENILE CONTACT CARD					5:57:1

Name: **Age:**   **Date of birth:**

Address:

**Previous address
(if recently moved):**

__*School/Employment:__

Place of interrogation: **Date/Time:**

Reason stopped:

Height	Hair	Eyes	Complexion	Build	Marks (scars, etc.)

In company with (1)

               (2)

*Delete if not applicable

W5765

Truant from school: YES/NO   If yes, indicate below action taken

Returned to school	YES/NO	Headmaster informed	YES/NO
Taken home	YES/NO	Parent/Guardian informed	YES/NO

Any other information:

_____

_____

_____

_____

_____

_____

Reporting Officer: **Div. No.**

Time and date of report: | Noted by Collator | Initials

Social Work (Scotland), Act, 1968, Part III—Reports of Crimes and Offences

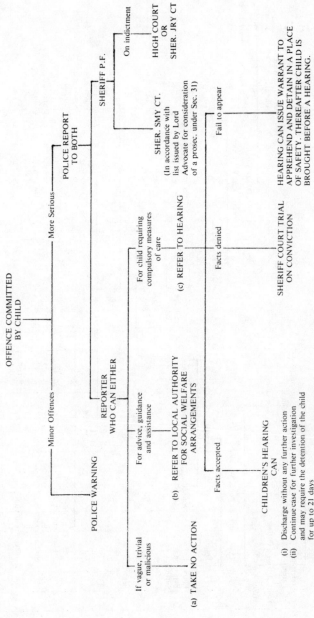

OFFENCE COMMITTED BY CHILD

Minor Offences / More Serious

POLICE WARNING

REPORTER WHO CAN EITHER

If vague, trivial or malicious

(a) TAKE NO ACTION

For advice, guidance and assistance

(b) REFER TO LOCAL AUTHORITY FOR SOCIAL WELFARE ARRANGEMENTS

For child requiring compulsory measures of care

(c) REFER TO HEARING

Facts accepted

CHILDREN'S HEARING CAN

(i) Discharge without any further action
(ii) Continue case for further investigation and may require the detention of the child for up to 21 days
(iii) Place the child under supervision (probation)
(iv) Place the child in a residential establishment

Facts denied

SHERIFF COURT TRIAL ON CONVICTION

POLICE REPORT TO BOTH

SHERIFF P.F.

SHER. SMY CT.
(In accordance with list issued by Lord Advocate for consideration of a prosec. under Sec. 31)

On indictment

HIGH COURT OR SHER. JRY CT

Fail to appear

HEARING CAN ISSUE WARRANT TO APPREHEND AND DETAIN IN A PLACE OF SAFETY. THEREAFTER CHILD IS BROUGHT BEFORE A HEARING.

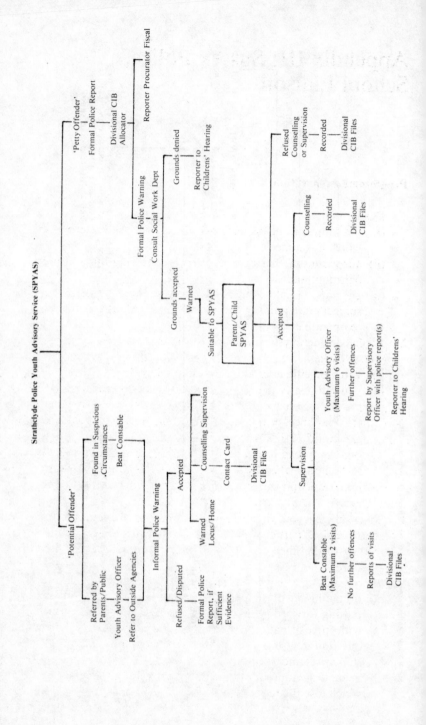

Strathclyde Police Youth Advisory Service (SPYAS)

Appendix III: Sussex Police, School Liaison

Programme Preparation

1. Ensure that:
   (i) the subject to be presented is suitable for the age group at which it is aimed;
   (ii) adequate time has been allotted for presentation and preparation; and
   (iii) any aids, visual or otherwise, are available to illustrate the subject matter and, if equipment is to be used, you are able to operate it satisfactorily.
2. When considering the suitability of subjects to be presented ask yourself whether
   (i) you are being used as a classroom relief for a teacher?
   (ii) you can justify the time and effort spent on preparation?
   (iii) the end result will be of value in creating a better understanding between yourself, teaching staff and students generally? If so, by accepting this particular subject to talk on, can it lead to establishing a more permanent link with the school, whereby you are able to deal with the more important and valuable subjects within your terms of reference?
3. Some subjects you will be required to present are complex and controversial, particularly if associated with subject matter relating to the liberty of the individual. The dangers in these cases are:
   (i) attempting to cover too much in too short a time;
   (ii) becoming involved in discussions in which you end up putting forward personal theories which may be in conflict with force or national policies. This is particularly so when questions relating to drink, drugs, pornography and censorship arise; and
   (iii) being drawn into areas of discussion with any one person which lose the rest of the class.

4. Ensure that when faced with a request to cover any particular subject that, if it falls within the category of 3 above, you allocate sufficient time to cover the subject correctly. It may be that it will be necessary to allocate a number of sessions to the subject, or deal with it as part of or as a whole term's project.
5. When formulating any programme with any school, ensure that a close liaison is maintained with the teaching staff, particularly those responsible for the classes with whom you are involved, as they are often only too pleased to advise and assist you in the best method of presenting your subject and to notify you of what visual aid equipment is available or otherwise.
6 Remember, you are a police officer going into a school with the permission of a head teacher. Whilst we often wish to extend our field of activities and specify the most pertinent subjects to be covered, initially we must accept the limitations placed upon us by this type of arrangement. As we gain the confidence of the teaching staff and the support for the work we are doing, we can then begin to initiate areas within which we would prefer to work as far as the long-term results of our efforts are concerned. This is why we often find ourselves initially in the position referred to in paragraph 2 above.

Activities within the schools, along broad lines could be divided into:

Ages 5-6   A policeman is a human being
Ages 7-8   Basic road safety, Green Cross Code
           Never go with strangers
Ages 8-10 Cycle proficiency, further road safety, introduction to various elements of police work and small class project
Ages 11-13 Expansion of 8-10 group work
           General involvement of schools liaison officer in their activities

1. Careers convention
2. Exhibitions
3. Whole field of community relations

Activities

1. SLOs will be guided by the needs of their individual head teachers
2. Expressed in different ways, degrees, schools
3. Activities already established
   Talks to pupils and staff on:
   (i) all aspects of police work
   (ii) Duke of Edinburgh Award Scheme, service, safety

(iii) Visits to police stations

(iv) Discussion groups on various subjects, e.g. law and order, citizenship, history

Objectives

1. Helping young people to face the problems and opportunities of adult citizenship (MAIN)
2. Specialists presentation of various departments and functions of the police
3. Main social problems e.g. violence and vandalism; truancy and delinquency

Types of Programmes

1. *Social Studies/Law and Order*
   (i) Policing this area—duties/training
   (ii) Accident prevention; accident investigation; traffic forensic science
   (iii) Visit to police station
   (iv) Policewomen's department; crime prevention; dogs; CID
   (v) Courts—juvenile courts; magistrates court; crown court
   (vi) Traffic department—vehicle examination; radar; abnormal loads; traffic control

2. *Project on Police History*

   (i) History of law and order to 1829
   (ii) History of police since 1829
   (iii) Man on the beat
   (iv) Police cars; police enquiry office; communications; PNC
   (v) 999 Calls; how and when; police action
   (vi) Specialist—CID; SOCO; policewomen; Fraud Squad; Diving Unit; CCTV; drugs

3. *Duke of Edinburgh Award*
4. *Pre-Driver Training*—West Sussex Liaison RSO
5. *Cycle Proficiency*—Liaison RSO Award
6. *Law Courts*
7. *Elementary Law*
8. *Police Systems* Comparison English Systems
9. *Police in Society*—Role; discipline
10. *Departments*—Specialist departments
11. *Road Safety*—Green Cross Code
12. *Water Safety*—Resuscitation

13. *Lower/Middle Schools*
    (i) Dangers in our Area—roads; ponds; rivers; quarries; building sites; railways; artillery ranges
    (ii) Safe and Sound—road safety projects incorporating Green Cross Code; dangerous spots in area
    (iii) Animals at Work—talk on the help the community and the police get from animals
    (iv) The Policeman—general look at policemen

14. *Middle Groups*
    (i) What do policemen do?—brief look at policemen
    (ii) *999 System—What Happens*—practical use of telephones
    (iii) *Police Through History*—can elaborate to two periods
    (iv) *Communication*—telephone to pictures in police car

15. *Upper Groups*
    (i) Police—how it works; what they do; visit police station
    (ii) *Courts Law of Justice*—how law is made; parliament; local authorities; features mock trial in hall or classroom
    (iii) *Children in Trouble*—a tactful look at theft, violence and vandalism
    (iv) *Observations and a First Look at Forensic*—practical work; slides; fingerprints
16. *The 999 System*—Sussex police organisation; function
17. *Role of the Policewoman*
18. *Policeman up-to-date*
19. *Accidents and Attitudes*
20. *Debates or Informal Group Discussion*—topical events in news appertaining to law and society
21. *Legislation*—how laws are made; voting
22. *The Law, your Rights*
23. *Forensic Science*
24. *The Police as a career*
25. *Forms of Communication*
26. *The Queen's Peace*—riots; protests; strikes; civil disobedience
27. *Careers Convention*

Appendix IV: Conclusions Extracted From Council of Europe Third Criminological Colloquium, 1978

Six Conclusions Drawn up by
General Rapporteur, Professor Michael Banton

1. Given that the protection of the public peace is of concern to all citizens, they should be aware of their obligations to its protection and not leave this responsibility in the hands of the police alone. Since the public needs educating in the changing nature of the problems it will assist if criminal policies are made explicit so that they can be widely debated.

2. The point of departure is the review of the criminal justice system as a whole. The public should be made aware of the costs of crime and of the institutions which respond to it so that they can have a better understanding of the results to be expected from alternative ways of spending the money which they contribute by taxation. As criminal policies become more explicit it will be easier to develop criteria for evaluating the performance of different institutions which should be concerned with crime prevention.

3. The criminal justice system needs to be seen from a broader perspective and any bodies established, nationally or locally, to review measures for the prevention of crime would include not only a wide range of official institutions (education, housing, health, planning, etc. as well as the police) but also private institutions like private security agencies and insurance companies.

4. As a way of giving more concrete expression to these general views, the European Committee on Crime Problems might draw the attention of member governments to the reports prepared in connection with the colloquium. Those countries which have not so far stressed the preventive function of their police might

examine the reports on the social role of the police with some care to see if it does not suggest to them ways in which their measures for prevention might be improved and the need for specialised police training in this field.

5.   The design of research into crime prevention in this area poses special problems and is hampered by the limitations upon communication between social scientists, police officers and civil servants. Consideration should be given to ways of bringing together in continuing dialogue those who have an interest in crime prevention research, so that strategies for research can be developed in which the police will cooperate and which will be related to the kinds of decisions that have to be reached by those holding political or administrative office.

6.   At present no country has a comprehensive strategy for crime prevention and even if one could be formulated immediately it would not be able for perhaps two decades to influence the tendencies which are making for an increase in criminality. Some countries have established national crime prevention councils but there may be advantages if different countries try different strategies, provided that information is exchanged about what initiatives prove successful and unsuccessful, and the reasons for this.

Select Bibliography

Alderson, J. *From Ideas to Resources* (Police Journal, 1977)
  'An Introduction to Probationary Constables on the Nature of
  Service in the Devon and Cornwall Constabulary' (unpublished
  paper)
Alderson, J. and Stead P. *The Police We Deserve* (1973)
Banton, M. *The Policeman in the Community* (Tavistock, 1974)
Belson, W.A. *The Police and the Public* (Harper & Row, 1975)
Bent, H.E. *The Politics of Law Enforcement* (Lexington Books,
  1974)
Boss, P. *Social Policy and the Young Delinquent* (Routledge and
  Kegan Paul, 1967)
Bordua, D.J. (ed.), *The Police; Sociological Essays* (Wiley, 1967)
Bright, J.A. 'The Beat Patrol Experiment' (unpublished report,
  July 1969)
Bruce, N. and Spencer, J. *Face to Face with Families* (Macdonald,
  1976)
Cain, M. 'Role Conflict among Police JLOs', *British Journal of
  Criminology* (1968), vol. 8, no. 4
Clarke, R. & Heal, K.H. 'Police Effectiveness in Dealing with
  Crime: Some Current British Research', *Police Journal* (1978),
  vol. LII, no. 1
Collier, P. 'The Policeman; Selection & Training', *Medico-Legal
  Journal* (1977), vol. 45, no. 1
Council of Europe, Third Criminological Colloquium, *The Police
  and the Prevention of Crime,* Report (1978)
Evans, P. *The Police Revolution* (Allen & Unwin, 1974)
Germann, A.C. 'Law Enforcement : a Look in the Future', *Police
  Journal* (October, 1977)
Grant, D. *The Thin Blue Line* (Long, 1973)
HMSO *Children in Trouble* (1968)
Hodges, J.J. 'Juvenile Offenders', *British Journal of Criminology*
  (1975), vol. 15, no. 4
Home Office Research Paper 8, *A Study of a Juvenile Liaison
  Scheme in West Ham* (1971)

Home Office Research Paper 34, *Crime as Opportunity* (1976)

Home Office Research Paper 37, *Police Cautioning in England & Wales* (1976)

Liverpool City Police *The Police and the Children* (1964)

Mack, J. 'Police Juvenile Liaison Scheme', *British Journal of Criminology* (April 1963), vol. 3, p. 361

Mack J. and Ritchie, M. *Juvenile Liaison* (University of Glasgow, 1968)

Mallion, D. 'The Police and the Community; a Scottish Survey', *Focus* (April 1974)

Martin, J.P. and Wilson, G. *The Police: A Study in Manpower* (Heinemann, 1969)

Michaels, R.A. and Treger, H. 'Social Work in Police Departments', *Social Work* (September 1973)

Mosse, G.L. (ed.), *Police Forces in History* (Sage, 1975)

Oliver, I. 'Metropolitan Police Approach to the Prosecution of Juvenile Offenders' (unpublished thesis, 1977)

Outram, M. *Evaluation of Police & Social Services Liaison Relating to Juveniles* (Cheshire Social Services Department, 1978)

Reiss, A.J. *The Police and the Public* (Yale, 1972)

Rose, G. and Hamilton, R.A. 'Effects of a JLO Scheme', *British Journal of Criminology* (1970), vol.10, no.1

Schaffer, E.B. 'The Police and Community Involvement', *Focus* (June 1972)

Scott, P. 'Childrens Hearings : a Commentary', *British Journal of Criminology* (1975) vol. 15, no. 4.

Scottish Home & Health Department *Police Warnings* (1945)

Scottish Home & Health Department *Report of the Working Party on Police Procedures Arising from Social Work (Scotland) Act, 1968* (1970)

Simpson, J. 'The Police & Juvenile Delinquency', *British Journal of Criminology* (1968), vol. 8, no. 2

Social Work in Scotland: Report by a Working Party on the Social Work (Scotland) Act, 1968 (Department of Social Administration, University of Edinburgh, 1969)

Strathclyde Police 'Youth Advisory Service' (unpublished paper)

Steer, D. *Police Cautions, a study in the Exercise of Police Discretion* Penal Research Unit, Occasional Paper 2, 1970)

Sundeed, R.A. 'Police Professionalisation and Community Attachments in the Diversion of Juveniles', *Criminology* (1974), vol. 11, no. 4

Terry, J. *Guide to the Children's Act* (Sweet & Maxwell, 1975)

Treger, H. 'Crime and Delinquency' in H. Treger, D. Thomson and G.S. Jaech *A Police-Social Work Team Model* (July 1974), pp.281-9

, 'Social Work in the Police Agency : Some Implications' (unpublished paper)

INDEX